The *Promise*
of
Barth

Also by Thomas C. Oden

Community of Celebration
Radical Obedience
Kerygma and Counseling
Contemporary Theology and Psychotherapy
The Structure of Awareness

The Promise of Theology
Martin E. Marty, General Editor

The Promise of Barth
The Promise of Bennett
The Promise of Bonhoeffer
The Promise of Buber
The Promise of Bultmann
The Promise of Heschel
The Promise of Kierkegaard
The Promise of H. Richard Niebuhr
The Promise of Reinhold Niebuhr
The Promise of Teilhard de Chardin
The Promise of Tillich

The Promise
of
Barth

The Ethics of Freedom

by
THOMAS C. ODEN

J. B. LIPPINCOTT COMPANY
Philadelphia and New York

*To three friends, through whose friendship has shone
the freedom of the Word:*

Pfarrer Adrian Geense, Heidelberg
Professor James M. Gustafson, Yale
Reverend Jackson McKinley Smith, Hingham,
  Massachusetts

Foreword

Fifty years before this book was written, a well-prepared Swiss pastor, Karl Barth, reacted in rage against shallow optimism in his commentary on St. Paul's letter to the Romans. More than rage was present in his writing, however. He helped Christian thought take a 180-degree turn, advocating God-centered instead of man-centered theology. Barth, in his own way, was always an extremist. He could write long tracts named simply *"No!"* to separate himself from men whose positions differed but slightly—so men had thought—from his own. His productivity, his dramatic flair, his love of paradox, his enjoyment of a kind of intellectual scandal all served to make him the first shaper of our century's theology.

They also worked to make him an object of attack and criticism. Those who help the pendulum swing can get hit hardest when it swings back. Late twentieth-century Christian thought, while it is not optimistic about man, is at least more man-directed than Barth's earlier tendencies had been. The liberalism he had shunned began to recover. The confidence he revealed in speaking about revelation and transcendence comes only with difficulty to a diffident, stumbling generation. Barth, once overpraised and overfeared, is now in danger of being overattacked by some or neglected by others.

Professor Oden, in the pages which follow, is not content merely with assessing Barth's place in theological history: it is undeniably large. He is concerned with helping readers find what may very well be overlooked during the years of reaction to some aspects of Barth's thought. Oden finds this in Barth's ethics. Now, it happens that in recent years the questions of personal and social responsibility and morality have come to the center once again. This book shows how ethical discourse can be clarified and intensified if Barth's sometimes overlooked promise is heeded. Oden, without dropping his critical guard, suggests that the proper response is not merely one of admiration. There is also the possibility that one should follow.

MARTIN E. MARTY
The University of Chicago

Acknowledgments

To Markus Barth I owe a special debt of thanks for a careful, critical reading of this discussion at an early stage, and for giving me the benefit of his penetrating comments. I am grateful for the pedagogy of Hans Frei of Yale University, who first awakened my interest in Barth's awesome *Dogmatik,* and who first opened the door for me to recognize the promise of Karl Barth amid rapid secularization. Above all I am indebted to my former colleague at Perkins School of Theology, John Deschner, for illuminating the special promise of Barth's thinking for an ethic of freedom.

Contents

The *Promise*
of
Barth

I.

Why Karl Barth?

A. A Personal Introduction

A *Journal Entry.* I know of no better way to intro-
duce Karl Barth than to share with you my journal entry of
October 8, 1965, when I met him in Basel:
"I had written Karl Barth previously that I would call when
I came through Basel on the way to Rome, inasmuch as I was
preparing a manuscript on his ethics and wanted to share with
him several perplexities. I called at his house in the morning,
only to find that, according to his grandson, he was in the
hospital and would not be home for another week. He suggested that I call anyway at the hospital to see if his grand-
father felt like receiving me. I did. He was very cordial and
I was astonished when he asked me to come to his hospital
room to visit with him at 4:00 P.M.

"After an exciting day at the Kunstmuseum, perusing the
famous modern art collection whose objectlessness Barth has
always disdained, I went out to the spare, ultra-modern city
hospital (Bergspital) where I was received promptly and
cordially. There was an elderly lady there who bade "Karl"
farewell as I entered, saying to me that he had told her he
was expecting me.

"First a description of the man—he was sitting in bed-
clothes and bathrobe in a chair beside his bed with a make-
shift desk made out of two hospital tables end on end. On
another smaller table there was a small shelf of books. The
only titles I recognized were Catton's *History of the Civil War*
and a volume of *Zeitschrift für Evangelische Ethik.*

"The most distinct instantaneous impression was of his wry smile, with his broken teeth, his famous pipe and bright, twinkly eyes. He radiated friendliness, depth, and warm personal interest in me.

"I had prepared three questions on a card which I gave him. The first was on the possible influence of volume II/2 of his dogmatics upon the development of Bonhoeffer's *Ethics* (1940–1943), or possibly vice versa. He answered firmly that he did not think the two works could be easily compared, since one was published posthumously in an unfinished form, and the other was a deliberate part of a larger systematic statement. But he seemed confident that Bonhoeffer had known nothing of his argument in II/2 before 1942 (I had thought otherwise). A bit argumentatively, I pointed out the remarkable similarity of their exegesis of Genesis 1–3 and their almost identical views of the concepts of command and obedience. I had suspected that Bonhoeffer had obtained the manuscript of II/2 prior to writing his essays. Barth admitted the similarity, but did not think Bonhoeffer had seen his argument in any form.

"My second query concerned the analogy of faith, the process of reasoning analogously from God's self-disclosure to human knowledge, in contrast to the traditional analogy of being, which reasons from the general concept of being to the being of God. I asked whether it might be applied to ethical reflection. I proposed that his discussion of analogy was relevant not only to a theory of knowledge and theological method (where he developed it), but also to the basic structure of ethics, i.e., we are called to act toward the neighbor as God has acted toward us, love as we have been loved, forgive as we have been forgiven, etc. 'Yes,' he answered, and cited his doctrine of marriage, asking if I thought it was clear there. I said only implicitly, not explicitly. Upon questioning, I explained my interest in the analogy of faith as a potential new basis for a theology of culture, as an alternative approach to

[16]

Tillich's theology of culture, which begins with man's existential questions and only then puts question to the Christian tradition about God's self-disclosure. His eyes were bright as he listened and nodded his head frequently, intently curious about my line of reasoning.

"He asked if I were interested as a theologian in dialoguing with the natural sciences. Yes. He warned that my only goal as a theologian should be to understand the Word of God. Briefly I summarized my argument on the relation of theology and psychotherapy, which I had developed in *Kerygma and Counseling*.

"This, in turn, led directly into my third question, which focused on the role of self-affirmation in Christian ethics. When he asked for clarification, I stated my conviction that all love of the neighbor is rooted in an appropriate self-affirmation, in response to God's affirmation of man. His face turned very serious for the first time, and intently he said: 'The self must give itself to the neighbor. You must not base Christian ethics upon self-affirmation or self-directed action of any sort. It is a very dangerous path and you should proceed very cautiously. The only source of love of the neighbor is the Word which God speaks affirming both you and the neighbor, and *not* in any self-affirmation which one gives to himself. The source of love always remains sheer gift and never is a possession by virtue of one's self-relation.' I asked if he understood Jesus' command to love others *as oneself* as implying self-love or self-affirmation. He replied that it completely denies self-affirmation. The love of the neighbor obliterates self-love. His position was very strong and forthright, and he seemed unwilling to give an inch. I was equally adamant and told him that my understanding of scripture as well as my experience with psychotherapy had made me strongly inclined to believe that there is no firm basis for self-giving without self-affirmation. But I agreed carefully to consider his admonitions. I then noted that I had taken enough of his time and was keenly aware of his physical limitations. He continued to question me about my work in the Psychiatric Department at Heidelberg and wondered of my concerns and intentions in my trip to Rome.

"As I prepared to leave the hospital, two of his statements imprinted themselves firmly on my memory. I can remember, upon explaining my proposal on the use of analogy to understand psychotherapy theologically, how intently and repetitiously he said: *"Probiere! Probiere! Probiere!"* (Try! Try! Try!), so as to affirm clearly, without committing himself to its consequences, my effort at a new concept of a theology of culture.

"Secondly, as I explained my views of the implicit theological assumptions of psychotherapy, he pointed out that in an era in which both theology and therapy are changing so rapidly, theology can only 'live by the Holy Spirit!' Those words sank deeply into my consciousness, due to the passionate stress he gave to them. He seemed to be saying that whatever awaits us in the emerging culture situation, the work we do as theologians can only properly be done in lively and contemporaneous response to the living Word of God which lays claim upon us in the present. This is why theology must constantly be re-done in response to God's ever newly occurring Word, yet once for all clarified in Jesus Christ.

"As I left I wished him good health from all his American friends, and reminded him of the remarkable contribution he had made to us all. He then said he was aware of his age, but in words most appropriate, which I cannot remember exactly, he said he was pleased to have lived a full life and was not complaining about these limitations. Throughout the whole conversation his manner was deeply joyous, alive, full of interest and concern and delight. As I left, he told me to greet the pope for him, and I replied I would greet them all in Rome on his behalf. With a little hand wave and a smile, I left him and closed the door. As I walked down the clean white halls of the hospital, I was deeply aware that I had met a truly great man and a great theologian of the church. We all stand on his shoulders in whatever we do."

That same evening, as I reflected on our conversation while in the little village of Biasco, Switzerland, I entered into my journal this act of thanksgiving:

For the celebrative smile through broken teeth,
the hearty clasp of time-worn hands,
unconscious of the powerful yeast they've molded,
for life lived mirthfully between the limits
of birth and death, God I am thankful.
For the miracle of radical accountability
hammering language out of gracious experience,
sharing in a community of celebration
embracing three millennia and more,
for quick minds seized by thy at-oneing deed,
for courage to risk to be oneself against the stream,
God I am thankful.

My friend, you have befriended me long before we met
to exchange penetrating glances.
Yet value it as I may, I am grateful less for our
fleet now of friendship than for the enduring
friendship of the One with whom we both now stand
in separation, for whom your life has danced and
strummed in rhythm with the end of time.

Barth's Pervasive Influence. For the better part of fifty years, the most powerful single voice in Protestant theology has been that of Karl Barth (rhymes with dart). Beginning with his commentary on Romans in 1919, some two hundred books and monographs have flowed from Barth's pen as well as innumerable essays on an immense variety of subjects from Mozart to Mariology.

Students from all continents have flocked to hear his lectures at the University of Basel, where he served as Professor of Theology from 1935 to 1962. His major work, *Die Kirchliche Dogmatik* (*Church Dogmatics*), has been referred to as "the most exhaustive compendium of what a Christian must believe, and why he believes it, that Protestantism has had in more than a century." [1] *

Almost every major figure in recent theology has disagreed with Barth, but all have been influenced by him. And although the current generation of younger theologians generally rejects any sort of scholastic Barthianism or neo-orthodoxy as passé, still they find themselves attracted to the scope and impressiveness of his work, his Christocentric humanism, and the consistency of his theological enterprise. Barth is regarded by some as the most important Protestant theologian since John Calvin and is frequently compared with such great religious thinkers as Augustine, Anselm, Luther and Schleiermacher, for like each of these, his work marks a new epoch in theology.

Barth is eulogized as one of the most significant innovators of Protestant history, but he himself was less concerned with creating something new than with listening seriously to the wisdom of the ancient Christian witness. Though well known as a consistent systematician, he abhorred rigid theological system-building and spoke of his own theological development as "a bird in flight."

Like the paradoxes which his theology plumbs, Barth as a man had many paradoxical features. If in his earlier period he spoke of God as "wholly other," later he wrote of "the humanity of God." Though he was for many years known chiefly for his low estimate of man's capacity, he later spoke of the special honor which God has done for man by himself entering into man's humanity, taking humanity upon himself in Jesus Christ. He has frequently been regarded as a pessimist yet he spoke more frequently and passionately of the Christian hope than any other theologian of his generation. Barth had harsh words for certain prevalent modes of pre-Vatican II Roman Catholic thinking, but he joyfully acknowledged that some of his best interpreters have been Catholics (notably Hans Küng and Hans von Balthasar).

While he is frequently classed with the philosophers of

* Superior figures refer to the Notes at the end of the text.

despair, he neither considered himself as a philosopher nor thought of his work as an act of despair, but, rather, as a most affirmative Yes toward man, whom God has created, claimed and reconciled. He was an ordained minister who called his chief work *Church Dogmatics*, but he delivered no sermons in his latter years except in the Basel jail to the prisoners, whom he affectionately called his "fellow sinners," earnestly awaiting the news of deliverance.

Even though we will often disagree with Barth, we cannot responsibly remain ignorant of him. If Barth's thought is a watershed in the history of theology, it is also a watershed in the history of ethics. It is ironic that a theologian who is dismissed so frequently on the basis of his lack of ethical relevance should have spent more time writing ethics and focused more on questions of ethics than any other major Protestant theologian of this century.

It is regrettable that Barth is sometimes associated in America with fundamentalist thought, for nothing could be further from the intent of his own theology than a kind of rigid, defensive biblicism which does not admit of critical study of the Scriptures. We tend to deal with Barth in terms of shorthand tags, like neo-orthodox, or Christomonist, but often these tags entirely fail to get to the heart of his intention. Many of the Barths which we have dismissed as irrelevant are fictitious straw men, the Barths of our imagination, a patchwork of fragmentary, hearsay reports.

Beyond all the diagnoses, prognoses and therapies of psychology and sociology and politics, Barth sought to speak of God's final intention and determination to give free grace to man. His concern centered upon the freedom of God for man, which enables the freedom of man for God. Listen all you can to the empirical examination of man as a historical or natural phenomenon. Let the psychologist, historian and philosopher reach to the full range of their competence, and in none of their reports about man will you ever hear this central assertion: Here is a being who is loved by God, created to be loved by God, to be the subject of God's gracious, reconciling action. It is on the basis of that distinctive presupposition that Barth proceeds to think about man as creature and his responsibility.

Karl Barth's death on December 9, 1968, marked the end of one of the most productive and controversial careers in the history of theology. He died in his sleep at his home in Basel at the age of eighty-two. It is the conviction and thesis of this book, however, that Barth's work is important not only for the past, or for the study of the history of theology, but also for the future. His life began a new epoch which is even yet awaiting fulfillment and full explication. He is relevant to our very situation today, in which his immense dogmatic is often impatiently dismissed as archaic and irrelevant.

The thesis of this whole series is that certain theologians of the recent "past" are well ahead of what is now going on in the present. Even though some regard them faddishly as passé, they are still the vanguard of the future, the most promising resources for our current situation. I intend to argue that case for Barth, especially with reference to his potential contribution to ethics, where he is often thought to be sadly deficient.

Since this brief study focuses on the *promise* of Barth's thought, I will not herein detail certain criticisms which I have elsewhere made of some of his limitations and internal inconsistencies as an ethicist. If the reader should wish to explore these, he may find them in a doctoral dissertation by the author on "The Idea of Obedience in Contemporary Protestant Ethics" (Yale, 1960).

B. The Background of His Thought

The Early Years. If Karl Barth is often considered a revolutionary, it is ironic that his style of revolution is a revolution through tradition, an attempt to recapture the revolutionary elements present in the Judeo-Christian tradition itself. That his revolution in theology was deeply embedded in the revolutionary spirit of Calvinist and Protestant reformers should not be surprising, since many of his ancestors were Swiss Reformed pastors and teachers.

Born on May 10, 1886, he was the eldest son of Fritz and Anna Barth. His father was a pastor in Basel. When he was three, his family moved to Bern, where Fritz Barth accepted a position in New Testament and church history at the University of Bern.

Karl Barth began the study of theology under his father's conservative tutelege in 1904, but two years later went to Berlin, the hub of liberal Protestantism, to study under the great church historian Adolf von Harnack. He also heard the lectures of Karl Holl (church history), Julius Kaftan (philosophy of religion), and Hermann Gunkel (history of religions), among the greatest theological scholars of Europe.

The young Barth followed enthusiastically Harnack's lectures on "The Essence of Christianity." Harnack was the culmination of the nineteenth-century liberal tradition from Friedrich Schleiermacher (who emphasized a theology of religious experience, focusing upon the feeling of absolute dependence) through Ritschl (who stressed value judgments in the knowing process and a strongly ethical religion). Harnack wanted to cut through the Hellenistic and medieval diversions and capture the simple teachings and personality of Jesus. He summarized the essence of Christianity under three headings: the kingdom of God, the infinite value of the human soul, and the commandment of love. Harnack epitomized the spirit of liberal optimism, assuming that man is essentially good and that history is getting better and better. It was against this naïve optimistic romanticism and the portraiture of Jesus as a bourgeois religious humanist that Barth's theology was later to rebel. But when he rebelled, it was against a stream in which he had been thoroughly immersed.

In 1908, after a summer in Tübingen, he received permission from his father to go to Marburg to study under the neo-Kantian philosophers Hermann Cohen and Paul Natorp, and above all the pre-eminent liberal systematic theologian, Wilhelm Herrmann, who was deeply concerned with ethical responsibility as a dimension of communion with God. Barth called Herrmann "*the* teacher of my student years." Although Barth later expressed his own theology in a very different way from his teacher, he nonetheless credited Herrmann with showing much of the path he was to follow. For implicit in Herrmann was an awareness of the absolute transcendence of God, a rejection of any scientific proof of God's existence, and the uniqueness of faith as the basis of theological reflection.

Ordained in 1908 in the Swiss Reformed Church, Barth worked for a short time as an assistant editor of *Die Christliche Welt*, the principal liberal journal of German Protestantism, rather similar to *The Christian Century*, under the editorship of Martin Rade, a friend of Harnack's. He then took his first pastorate, in Geneva, from 1909–1911.

It is worth noting that Barth was not preparing to be a teacher of theology but to be a parish minister. He did indeed spend over ten years, 1911–1921, as pastor of a small church in the remote village of Safenwil in Aargau, Switzerland. It was directly out of his struggle to minister to his congregation and to preach to them faithfully that the theological revolution of our times was born.

This parish was itself involved in rapid social transformation. Safenwil contained a sawmill, a dye factory and a weaving plant. Barth became interested in the fate of the workers in a society struggling from rural patterns to industrialization. It was there that he and his friend Eduard Thurneysen, who pastored in a neighboring village, became religious socialists. Barth supported the factory workers in their struggle for better working conditions. So active was he in the cause of religious socialism that he was nicknamed by his disturbed congregation the "red pastor." He tried to organize unions for the poorly paid textile workers and refused to recognize the distinction between rich and poor. As a member of the Social Democratic Party, along with Paul Tillich and others, he felt that the socialist movement was a cause of great religious importance, destined to become an instrument for realizing God's kingdom on earth, following the thinking of Herrman Kutter and Leonhard Ragaz.

The Break with Liberalism. It was World War I, and especially the weak response of religious liberals to the war, which undermined his previous optimism. He became painfully aware that the romanticist assumptions of idealistic socialism could not withstand certain demonic temptations. The vague hopes of liberal humanism seemed overwhelmed by the thundering guns of war. The specific turning point for Barth was that "black day" when ninety-three German intellectuals announced their support of the war policies of Kaiser Wilhelm II. Barth realized to his horror that even some of his theological teachers, whom he had so greatly respected, were among this group. He wrote: "I suddenly realized that I could not any longer follow either their ethics and dogmatics or their understanding of the Bible and of history."

He discussed his doubts with his friend Eduard Thurneysen, and found in him a kindred spirit. These two young pastors initiated a profound, far-reaching correspondence which involved a thoroughgoing critical review of the theological constructs they had received. When Barth read Christoph Blumhardt on pastoral care, his understanding of the Christian hope became redirected toward the absolutely transcendent God, instead of hope for historical progress and human good will. He began to be suspicious of the tendency of religious socialism to reduce Christianity to a political movement and to allow the gospel to be absorbed into limited cultural forms.

It was precisely amid this struggle to preach faithfully to his congregation that Barth found it necessary to return to historical study to re-evaluate the theological resources he had been bequeathed. The momentous turning point came when Barth turned to the study of Paul, beginning a careful, painstaking exegesis of the Epistle to the Romans. To his astonishment, a radically new understanding of reality began to dawn upon him, a revolutionary theocentrism which consistently viewed human reality from the viewpoint of God's own encounter with it. Although he did not at first intend to publish his exegesis, he later prepared it for submission, and the first edition of *Romans* was published in 1919.

Later he likened himself to "one who, ascending the dark staircase of a church tower, and trying to steady himself, reached for the banister, but got hold of the bell rope instead. To his horror, he had then to listen to what the great bell had sounded over him, and not over him alone." [2] The bell which Barth had rung resounded throughout Protestant theological circles, and ultimately throughout the whole world. Famous overnight, he soon received an invitation from Göttingen University to take a chair in systematic theology paid for by funds from Reformed Churches in America.

Nineteenth-century liberal theology had tended to reduce revelation to history, science and philosophy. The infinite qualitative difference between God and man had been erased. Barth spoke of God as "wholly other," over against all human finitude and pride. He called the Christian to risk himself in the leap of faith to embrace the yea-saying of God, beyond all the No's of life. He spoke of revelation not as an idea or abstract truth to which one gives his assent, but as the event of God's own self-disclosure in history, an occurrence with cosmic relevance, God's own entry into history.

In his earlier period, Barth felt a close kinship to Søren Kierkegaard, who had also struggled against a diluted Christendom, who spoke of faith as a scandal to reason, and who would not allow any sentimental or philosophical access to Christian faith. He said the only system he knew was the Kierkegaardian affirmation of the "infinite qualitative difference between God and man." It was on a Kierkegaardian basis that he proposed to effect a turn in theology of "exactly 180 degrees," from a humanistic, optimistic trust in man's moral omnicompetence to a decisive affirmation of the competence of God to reconcile himself to man and make himself known.

This is what, as Catholic theologian Karl Adam said, "fell like a bombshell on the playground of the theologians."[3]

During the 1920's, Barth edited an influential journal called *Zwischen den Zeiten*. The title, translated "Between the Times," referred to the understanding of history which characterized its viewpoint—the contributors understood themselves to be standing between the times of God's encounter with man in Jesus Christ and the finalities of history, and more immediately between the times of the dissolution of an old era of history and the emergence of a new one. Many major figures engaged in a thoroughgoing critique of liberal theology on its pages. The list of contributors reads like a Who's Who of twentieth-century theology: Emil Brunner, Friedrich Gogarten, Karl Hein, Rudolf Bultmann and Eduard Thurneysen.

Barth had been at Göttingen only four years when he was invited to the chair of theology at the University of Münster. His commentary on Romans went through seven printings, each one with a new preface. It was translated into English in 1933 and has been one of the most widely read books on exegesis in the history of Christianity.

It is understandable that those who associate with liberalism a strong ethical emphasis, would also associate with Barth's polemic against liberalism a corresponding nonethical disinterest, or an atrophy of ethical concern. It is our intention to show that such is not the case. Even in his earliest writings of the 1920's amid his great struggle with liberalism, and continuing throughout his whole career, the central questions of ethics (behavior, decision, love, responsibility, action, intention, will) were at the heart of his concern. His emphasis on God's electing grace and love for man does not imply that he thereby de-emphasizes man's responsible answer to that grace. There is no lack of attention to the demand for concrete behavioral changes in response to God's gracious action. Barth was concerned with human action in the light of and in response to the predisposing determination of God's action.

Despite the fact that Kierkegaard was becoming increasingly

[27]

popular, Barth dropped him more and more to the edge of his reflection. By 1949, when he published a famous study on nineteenth-century Protestant theology, there is hardly the slightest mention of Kierkegaard's name.

The "mature Barth" began to emerge in the late twenties in connection with his intensive work on Anselm. In 1931 Barth wrote a short book entitled *Fides Quaerens Intellectum* (Faith Seeking Intelligibility), a study of Anselm's theological method. He argued that Anselm's theistic argument must not be interpreted as a strictly objective, rationalistic argument for the existence of God addressed to the non-faithful, but, rather as the reasoning of a faithful medieval believer. During this period he began to think about knowledge of God on the basis of a totally different style of analogical thinking, which he called *analogia fidei* (the analogy of faith); it moves from the reality of God to human realities, instead of moving in the pattern of the classical *analogia entis* (the analogy of being) which moves from the general concept of being to the being of God.

Earlier, in 1927, Barth had made his first attempt at the writing of a systematic theology in the untranslated *Christ-liche Dogmatik* (Christian Dogmatics), but no sooner was it published than Barth decided its approach was completely inadequate. It was his study of Anselm which forced him to leave this work unfinished and turn to the writing of his major work, *Church Dogmatics* (1932–1968). Most of the references we shall make in this study will be to this remarkable work of the "mature Barth." Barth's reputation as a theologian rests largely upon this massive work, which has expanded over a period of thirty-five years to over six million words on more than 7,000 pages in thirteen volumes, and it was even then left unfinished. The title was carefully chosen, however, and is indicative that Barth sees the task of theology as firmly grounded in the existence and reality of the believing Christian community and that object which it believes and remembers, namely, the action of God. Dogmatics, according to

Barth, is a self-critical investigation of human speech which seeks to point to God's own speech, to make our human language responsive to God's self-disclosure. Theology, for Barth, is above all a "joyful science" in which the pleasure and joy of our being claimed and known by God is the central focus of a scientific inquiry.

The immensity of this work has been the subject of a great deal of spoofing, in which Barth himself participated. On one occasion Barth wrote: "The angels laugh at old Karl. They laugh at him because he tries to grasp the truth about God in a book of Dogmatics. They laugh at the fact that volume follows volume, and each is thicker than the previous one. As they laugh, they say to one another, 'Look! Here he comes now with his little pushcart full of volumes of the Dogmatics!' And they laugh about the men who write so much about Karl Barth instead of writing about the things he is trying to write about. Truly, the angels laugh." [4]

The German Church Struggle. In 1933 the Nazis tried to unite the varying elements of Protestant leadership under the guidance of Ludwig Müller, who was handpicked by Adolf Hitler to manage the "German Christian" movement. In 1930 Barth had moved to Bonn to teach in the chair of theology, where he watched these developments with keen interest. When the German Christians began to try to force the Nazi deification of the German state upon the churches, Barth rebelled. As a university professor, Barth was himself a civil servant. He refused to take the oath of allegiance which Hitler required of all employees of the state. He also refused to begin his lectures with a salute to the Führer. The battle lines were set.

In 1934 the Barmen Synod was called. The best leadership of German Protestantism gathered to discuss the new situation. Barth was the chief author of the famous "Barmen Confession" which grew out of that synod and was signed by some two hundred leaders of "The Confessing Church." It is a declaration of the freedom of the church from all temporal interference. It asserts that the church has no other authority but the word of God in Jesus Christ. The implication is clear that the idolatrizing of the Nazi state could never be harmonized with Christian belief. Those who sometimes think of Barth as "politically disinterested," or as disengaged in the realities of contemporary history, need only look at the story of his risky political involvement during these times for a model of political confrontation.

Shortly after Barmen, Barth was condemned by a Nazi court as "seducing the minds" of his students, and was dismissed from his teaching position at Bonn. On November 27, 1934, he was escorted to the Swiss border and expelled from Germany.

In 1938 Barth was given the high honor of being invited to give the Gifford Lectures at Aberdeen University. In his commentary on the Scottish Confession of 1560, he further developed his theology of politics, and the relation of witness and service. He asserted that "Jesus Christ is Lord not only of the Church but also of the world." [5]

When Chamberlain went to Munich to discuss the fate of Czechoslovakia with Hitler, Barth wrote an oft-quoted letter to his former student, Joseph Hromadka: "The liberty of the whole of Europe, and maybe not only that of Europe, depends on the liberty of your people." Urging resistance to the Nazis, he wrote, "Still I dare hope that the sons of the old Hussites will show weakened Europe that even today there are still real men. Every Czech soldier who will fight or suffer will do this also for us. Today I even make bold to add without any reservation: he will do it also for the Church of Jesus Christ." [6]

Barth's reasons for opposing Nazism were essentially theological and not in a specific sense political. He understood Nazism under the categories of heresy and idolatry, not under the categories of imperialism and self-aggrandizement. He spoke of Nazism as a systematic transgression of the First Commandment. Barth especially resisted the "Aryan paragraph" of the German Christians, according to which Christians of Jewish origin were not allowed full participation in the Christian community. In the final analysis, however, Barth's theological rejection of Nazism hinged on its anti-Semitism, wherein "the Christian church is attacked at its very root and threatened with death. . . . Anti-Semitism is sin against the Holy Spirit." [7]

Later, when he tried to return to Germany shortly before the outbreak of hostilities, he was once again arrested and deported by the Nazis. He returned to Basel and spent the remainder of his life there. Although he had always been interested in military history, Barth had never served in the military, partly because of his poor eyesight. At the age of fifty-four he volunteered to serve in the auxiliary corps of the Swiss Army and did sentry duty on the Swiss border.

Though he opposed Nazism as basically anti-German, he spoke up strongly after World War II of his sympathy for the German people, and he admonished those who would nurse destructive feelings of hatred toward the Germans. When he returned to Germany as guest professor at the University of Bonn, he protested the vindictive spirit of the allied conquerors and argued that political freedom of the postwar German people was the only basis upon which they could grow toward responsibility and hope.

Communism and Anti-Communism. Some of Barth's critics, such as Reinhold Niebuhr and Emil Brunner, have been amazed that Barth would express such passionate resistance to Nazism, yet take a position of neutrality in the Cold War. A careful examination of his reasoning will show that his position was not, as Niebuhr implied, simply frivolous or without principle, but was actually an expression of the very evangelical freedom that he had been attempting to communicate from the beginning of his theological efforts.

To the surprise of many of his friends, Barth refused to condemn Soviet imperialism in Eastern Europe. He argued that Communism, quite unlike Nazism, had a totally materialistic world-view which did not threaten the internal authenticity of the church. Its atheism is to be contrasted with the idolatrous pseudo-messianism of the Nazi regime. Although he did regard Communism as idolatrous, he saw it more as a by-product of the failure of Western Christianity to solve its problems. He was more deeply concerned about the religious anti-Communism of the American McCarthy period, which was so presumptuous as to identify Christianity with Western and particularly American values. He urged his fellow churchmen in East Germany not to take Communist atheism as seriously as it takes itself. ". . . you should accept none of your countrymen at their own estimate. Don't ever honor them as the unbelieving and strong men they pretend to be! . . . They are just posing as the strong men they would like to be! Rather, you must meet their unbelief with a joyous unbelief in their attempted atheism. You as Christians must confidently claim that your atheists belong to God as much as you do. . . . What is certain is that God is not against them, but for them." [8]

Barth stubbornly refused to allow himself to be identified as a partisan in the Cold War. He wondered if the bold, open atheism of Russian Communism might not be actually easier for the church to deal with than the hidden, secretive, factual atheism of Western anti-Communist materialism. While Niebuhr and Brunner took up strong anti-Communist positions, Barth refused even to condemn the Russian invasion of Hungary. Later he said, "I am glad that I do not have to live within the sphere of influence of Communism and I wish that no one be forced to do that." Yet he argued that anti-Communism as a principle seems to be an even greater evil than Communism itself. Barth always distrusted the armaments race and especially the way the Western "Christian" powers have viewed themselves as the angels of light and the Communists as the demonic forces. Instead of identifying themselves uncritically with the materialistic West, the churches should have proclaimed the gospel of peace and reconciliation and expectation of the kingdom of God.

[32]

To charges of inconsistency, he answered that the church does not speak or act "on principle," but, rather, judges individual cases situationally. It is free to travel new paths and is not bound simply to casuistic principles. It is free to respond to the word, the claim, the command of God as it is presenting itself in contemporary history. "Communism, as distinguished from Nazism, has not done, and by its nature cannot do, one thing: It has never made the slightest attempt to reinterpret or falsify Christianity, . . . or to shroud itself in a Christian garment . . . and it has never committed the crime of anti-Semitism." [9]

In Barth we have a strongly historical conception of Christian political action, one which is concretely responsive to occurring history instead of some general overarching law or political principle. This is why Barth's political views tend to have a confessional and crisis character.

The Critics. Barth's stormy career has never been without the benefit of serious criticism. From the very beginning he has been attacked on every side by those who sensed that his theology was a threat to their dearest assumptions. Brunner, for example, who worked alongside Barth in an earlier period, and agreed with him on many points, refused to accept his rejection of natural theology, in their famous debate in 1931 on whether the natural man has a "point of contact" with God. Brunner was arguing that man must have some point of contact even to be able to know that he has received revelation. Against this, Barth wrote his famous *No!*, saying that God not only reveals himself to man but provides also the potentiality for man to receive that revelation as sheer grace. The central issue for Barth was that no knowledge of God is innately given in man's natural condition, that God is known at the point where he makes himself known, and that that point is Jesus Christ.

Fundamentalists have attacked Barth on his view of the Bible. For Barth, the Bible *per se* is not the word of God; Jesus Christ is the Word of God. He valued the written word highly, but that did not mean, as for many fundamentalists, that Scripture should not be subjected to intense historical-critical scrutiny. One of the tragedies of the importation of Barth's view of revelation into American theology is that it has suffered from a confused association with American fundamentalism, with which it differs profoundly.

Paul Tillich was among the early critics who charged that Barth was not allowing human culture to raise its own questions for theology. Barth replied that theology does not begin with the questions that human culture frames, but, rather, it reframes the questions of human culture. Against Tillich's charge that he was not leaving enough room for philosophy and for the humanistic sciences, Barth answered that philosophy has only a limited role to play in theological reflection. Admittedly some kind of language which may utilize philosophical concepts is inevitable for Christian proclamation, but the church must not ever allow its message to become entrapped in a single philosophical system (as he felt Bultmann had allowed existential philosophy to predominate in his thinking).

The Bultmannians have criticized Barth on the grounds that he has been too willing archaically to use biblical language and not try to relate it to the situation today. Yet Barth has never been quite so interested in man's communication to man as he has been in God's communication to man, God's own self-disclosure of his Word. He has consistently argued that man must be grasped by God's own self-communication before he can understand how he is called upon to communicate to his fellow man.

Barth against Barthianism. Despite heavy criticism, Barth came through this storm of theological conflict with a sparkling sense of humor, and responded in new ways to new historical situations. Even in his sixties and seventies, he was still undergoing significant changes. In 1956 he addressed a group of Swiss theologians on the subject of the humanity of God. At that time he felt it necessary to correct some of the exaggerations which were present in the earlier emphasis upon the infinite qualitative difference between God and man. In "The Humanity of God" he talked about the way God has become man, shared in our humanity, and therefore honored all humanity. There is in the Christian faith a profound Christian humanism, or more specifically, God's own humanism, God's own humanity and engagement in the flesh.

To everyone's surprise, Barth undertook a trip to the United States after his retirement in 1962 at the age of seventy-five to receive an honorary doctorate from the University of Chicago, where his son Markus was a teacher of New Testament. Thousands came from long distances to hear these lectures, in which Barth outlined an introduction to evangelical theology, speaking of the task of the theologian. His theme was the freedom of theology. During his visit to America he surprised many with his brilliant repartee and wit. He attended some nightspots in Chicago, listened to the satire of the Second City Players, and in general seemed to break the mold of the expectation many people had of him that he was sour on humanity.

It has been said that Barth looked like a casting agency's idea of a German professor, with his shock of wavy gray hair, high forehead and cheekbones, craggy eyebrows. His owlish eyes peered occasionally over his horn-rimmed glasses, which often sat at the tip of his nose. He was known for his geniality, modesty, patience and sympathy, and above all a pixyish sense of humor. Long a student of military history, he became a Civil War buff, and during his trip to America visited many of its battlefields.

Karl Barth married Nelly Hoffman, a musician, in 1913, and they had four children: Markus, who is now a New Testament professor at Pittsburgh Theological Seminary; Christoph, who teaches Old Testament at the University of Indonesia in Jakarta; Franziska, who married a businessman from Basel; and Matthias, who died in a mountain-climbing accident.

A passionate admirer of Mozart, for years Barth had begun

[35]

and ended his day with Mozart recordings. During the bicentennial celebration of Mozart's birth in 1956 he wrote a short book entitled *Wolfgang Amadeus Mozart* in which he discussed the theme of freedom in this great composer. "If I ever go to heaven," he said, "I would first of all inquire about Mozart, and only then about Augustine, Thomas, Luther, Calvin, and Schleiermacher."

His last years were replete with numerous illnesses and hospital recuperations. In September, 1966, he was able to attend a congress of Catholic theologians in Rome, where he had an interview with Pope Paul VI and subsequently wrote an account of his journey and his conversation with Rome in its postconciliar situation.

It is ironic that, despite its importance and widely acknowledged significance, the *Church Dogmatics* is not being widely read in our own time. It is clear that any sort of rigid, slavish Barthianism is archaic and uninteresting to the emerging generation of theologians. Yet it is equally clear that Barth did not want to make disciples; he only wanted to provide a fund of reflection upon which others could do their own thinking. He told his students: "Don't repeat what I have said; learn to think for yourselves." He was constantly moving "against the stream." The thirteen immense volumes of the *Church Dogmatics* may seem like an obstacle to communication, yet one may be assured that in the years ahead anyone who studies Protestant theology will certainly study the work of Karl Barth, and indeed he may be read in the future with greater intensity than he is being read in the present. We now turn to the special promise of Barth's thought for the current situation.

C. Barth as Ethicist

The Promise of Karl Barth: Eight Issues. Our thesis: Barth holds special promise for us today precisely at the point at which he is most frequently dismissed, i.e., his ethics, his understanding of the Christian life, Christian freedom and ethical responsibility. Eight areas of surprising relevance deserve our attention at first. In each case they will be treated more fully in the subsequent chapters.

(1) Western society of the 1970's will struggle desperately with the concept of *freedom*. Both young and old, both the political left and right, East and West, both secularist and religionist, black and white—all are now asking and will continue to ask what it means to embody freedom in political structures, in personal life, and in interpersonal relationships. Psychotherapy is profoundly concerned with the question of the liberation of man from neurotic conflict. Both the severest critics and the stanchest defenders of American society take as their theme "freedom." If young and old are devoted to any one concept, it is this one, however unclear we may be about its meaning or ground.

Yet we find ourselves, as a society, caught in profound moral perplexities just at the point of our quest for freedom. Many forms of bondage persist within our society, some of which have emerged precisely out of the malaise of our very concept of freedom. It is just at the point of re-examining the basic concept of freedom that I find Barth's ethic profoundly suggestive for our particular situation.

The hippies and young nonconformists are already teaching us a great deal about the courage to *be* free. One might expect that such a viewpoint would find no kinship whatever with a dogmatic theologian of the Calvinist tradition, but I see Barth as more profoundly associated with this sort of quest for authentic human freedom than any theologian of our time. The freedom of God for man, and the corresponding freedom of man for God and for all others, is the core theme of Barth's ethic. It was not an inadvertent slip when he described his mature theology as "a theology of freedom." [10]

(2) Another dimension of our current social situation to which Barth speaks in a promising way concerns the dialogue between freedom and *law*. In our emerging political situation

"law and order" will continue to be a divisive issue. Barth has offered us a far more profound dialectic between Christian faith and the law than have alternative discussions. Artists, therapists and avant-garde church renewalists are all struggling against a narrow, legalistic conception of human responsibility. In their efforts to liberate man from legalism, they find a curious ally in Karl Barth, whether they wish to listen to him or not. But on the other hand, there are those who are profoundly concerned with the maintenance of law, and the meaning of law from the perspective of the gospel and God's action in Jesus Christ. These people will also find significant insights in Barth's unique reformulation of the dialectic between gospel and law.

(3) *The crisis in authority* is a fundamental dilemma of our times. Almost every young person attempting to stand responsibly in the modern period is struggling with this question in some form. It is just amid this crisis in authority that Barth's conception of the command of God as *permission* speaks with profound relevance. The authority of the command of God lies precisely in its permission, that we become who we are. This is a very subtle dialectic, typical of Barth's discussion of freedom, which well deserves to be carefully studied by both younger and older generations.

(4) Modern men often find themselves trapped in *multiple conflicting obligations*. Little help is to be found in the moralistic tradition of Christian ethics for these dilemmas, since the emphasis there lies in constantly increasing the weight of the moral demands.

Even though we think of ourselves as a permissive society, not so terribly concerned with moral obligation, the force of multiple simultaneous demands upon our consciousness has not been relieved, and in fact may have been increased by the sophistication of electronic communication media. It is to just this situation of intensifying crisis in conflicting obligations that Barth's ethics so creatively speaks. For he is providing us with a new formula, a fresh statement, a different set of categories, a unique interpretive structure for dealing with multiple simultaneous obligations in a way that men will find liberating.

(5) Another area in which we seem to have come to a dead end in Protestant theology is the question of the possibility of *God language*. Following the Necro-theologians, many younger critics have assumed that Barth least of all would have anything to say to them, since he has relied so heavily upon traditional God language.

It is precisely into this situation that Barth's rather limited, modest style of theologizing may come to have immense importance. In my judgment, the most incisive criticisms of religion by Feuerbach, Nietzsche and Freud can be more meaningfully and directly assimilated into Barth's theology than in most of its alternatives. For despite the fact that he continued to employ traditional God language and to point confidently to the reality of God, Barth affirmed some of the most decisive criticism of anthropocentric views of "God." He can readily agree with Feuerbach that most of our language about "God" is merely a projection of our human needs. In fact, Barth says, much of the history of talk about "God" has been little more than just that. This is because God is known only where he makes himself known. If any language about God is possible at all, it is possible only in response to his actual self-disclosure, his own speech about himself in history. Here we have a strongly self-limiting style of theologizing, and one which remains surprisingly appropriate to man's secularizing context, affirming and celebrating that context. Barth, of course, is the father of Bonhoeffer's ideas of "religionless Christianity." That Barth's theology can speak to the secularizing context as well or better than its alternatives is clearly evidenced by the fact that his theology has been more meaningfully assimilated and utilized in the Eastern zone of Europe, amid an overtly atheistic context, than have the views of any other recent theologians.

(6) Another point at which Barth has surprising relevance

is in the current discussion of *situation ethics*. Why has this become such a disputed popular issue? Partly because of the sexual revolution. When parents of college students think of "situation ethics" they normally associate that term with sexual experimentation, trial marriage, the pill, and so on. But "situation ethics" is not related only to the discussion of popular sexual morality; it also remains a serious issue for theoretical ethics. A part of the failure of popular situation ethics, as seen for example, in the work of Joseph Fletcher, is its tendency to abstract the situation from the question of memory, to divorce the special context from any overarching interpretation of history. Thus "the situation" becomes abstract. It is taken out of its historical context. The debate on situation ethics has generally been a discussion of the relationship between rules or principles, on the one hand, and contexts, on the other. Barth enters that arena with a certain perspective which helps it through some of its most prevalent pitfalls. Barth is a situation ethicist in the sense that he has been profoundly concerned with how the present situation presents and embodies the claim of God. But he interprets "the situation" theologically and Christocentrically in such a way that the whole concept of situation ethics is transformed. A careful reappropriation of Barth's ethic should call for a serious reformulation of the questions being raised in situation ethics, and in that respect I find the ethical thought of Barth most promising.

(7) Another arena in which Barth's ethical thought is seminal is the question of *secularity* and in general the whole understanding of creation and "the world." A theological interpretation of the saeculum (the world, this age) is perhaps *the* fundamental issue of the post-Bonhoeffcrian period. We cannot ignore the path which Barth and Bonhoeffer have set. We must deal seriously with "the world" as a theological construct. The Christian community cannot consider the world apart from Jesus Christ, nor Jesus Christ apart from the world. Theologians have come to a serious crisis in this discus-

sion. Some have tended to think autonomously and non-theologically about the secularizing process. We are greatly tempted to reflect upon secularization simply in secular ways, failing to apply a genuinely theological critique of secularization. One of the most promising aspects of a reappraisal of Barth's ethics in the next decade may be to ask seriously how we can understand the reality of the world before God as created and redeemed. That question is thoroughly explored in Barth's doctrine of creation, and it has profound ethical consequences which we shall explore.

(8) One final area for which Barth may have profound promise is on the question of *man*, the definition of man, true humanism, and a truly hopeful understanding of man. Like secularity, we have considered "man" as a very abstract concept, abstracted out of his relationship to the creative and reconciling action of God. We can learn a great deal from Barth about a reaffirmation of man from the perspective of God's affirmation of him.

Admittedly, there may be many other dimensions of Barth's promise and relevance than those we discuss here. His work certainly has a great deal of continuing relevance for the study of the biblical witness, the doctrine of God, the question of the church's mission, and eschatology, but we must limit our scope. We are focusing on how Barth holds special promise for us at precisely that point where he is most frequently dismissed, that is, in his concept of Christian life and evangelical freedom, which is the center of his theological and social ethics.

A New Look at Barth's Ethics. One sometimes wonders if those who dismiss Barth's ethical thinking are actually aware of how extensively he has written in the area of ethics. It is probably correct to say that Barth has attended to questions of ethics more than Tillich, certainly more than Bultmann, and a great deal more than more recent theologians like Heinrich Ott, Gerhard Ebeling, Schubert Ogden, Wolfhart Pannenberg and others. Only Reinhold Niebuhr, among theologians

[41]

of his own generation, has been as deeply committed as a theologian to discussing questions of concrete ethics. In Barth we have not only one full volume of the *Dogmatics*, but many other subsections of the *Dogmatics* which are devoted to questions of general and special ethics. I would estimate that no less than two thousand pages of the *Church Dogmatics* alone are devoted specifically to ethical issues, and in addition there are many other occasional essays. One reason that Barth is not thought of as an ethicist is that he has never published, like Helmut Thielicke or Emil Brunner, a single separate book on ethics, as if it could be divorced from his *Dogmatics*.

In focusing on Barth's ethical reflection as the heart of his promise for the future of Christian thought, we are certainly not in agreement with the majority opinion which has tended to regard the ethical side of Barth as his weaker side. It cannot be our purpose in such a brief discussion to review in any detail the extensive criticisms which have been made of Barth's ethics, yet suffice it to say that this has been a recurrent criticism made by a wide variety of commentators over two generations.

Merely to provide the briefest sampling of this criticism: Barth's ethics have been charged with "a lack of historicity," "a monistic and timeless tendency," with becoming a "divine monologue" (Thielicke), with "hyper-objectivism" which "makes this contemporary situation of the Church unintelligible" (R. R. Niebuhr), "lack of historical sophistication," "theological-ethical nonsense," "a great deal of confusion about casuistry" (Fletcher).[11]

John Baillie and others have protested Barth's "radically mistaken dichotomy" between faith and history.[12] Thielicke has suggested that Barth's ethics are "exposed in large measure to the danger of passing theological judgments on democracy and totalitarianism which are not derived from the true center of theological ethics, but are based rather on political . . . and sometimes even purely Swiss, considerations. . . ."[13] According to R. R. Niebuhr, Barth's "ultra-realism" tends to become "oblivious of the actual Christian community." [14] John Cobb has argued that Barth is not seriously interested in "an encounter between the divine Person and the human person." [15]

No one has put the case against Barth's ethics more power-fully and influentially than Reinhold Niebuhr, who has harshly judged Barth's political decisions "an amateur intru-sion of absolute religious judgments into the endless relativ-ities of the political order." The center of Niebuhr's criticism is what he calls Barth's "extreme pragmatism, which disavows all moral principles." Niebuhr has taken Barth's ethics to task for refusing "to make discriminating judgments about good and evil if the evil shows only one horn or half of a cloven foot." [16]

Admittedly, any discussion of Barth's critics could be ex-tended almost indefinitely, since virtually everyone has taken his own special pot shot at Barth's "excessive Christomonism" or "archaic neo-orthodoxy." It is at least clear that Barth's *ethics* has been received much less affirmatively than his the-ological work as a whole.

It thus seems desirable for us to review the central theme of his ethics of freedom, if for no other reason than to see what others have most severely criticized. Sometimes one won-ders, however, whether the critics have really taken the mature work of Barth as seriously as the early Barth of the 1920's. There seems to be an irresistible hunger for caricature in most of these thumbnail critiques.[17] All that we have said up to this point is merely a prelude to the heart of our discussion, which will center on the freedom of God for man, and the freedom of man for God and the neighbor.

II.

Christ's Obedience and Ours

A. God's Taking Responsibility for Man

The Obedience of Jesus Christ in Our Place. Obedience to God has already occurred (*ist schon geschehen!*),[1] according to Barth. This is the unalterable beginning point of Barth's ethic: the obedience of Jesus Christ in our place. Everything hinges on the presupposition that man's proper response to God has taken place already in the response of the Son of God, and that man is called to determine himself in correspondence with this good news. Our assessment of Barth's promise for contemporary Christian thought must take focus here rather than at some peripheral point.

The fitting and appropriate action of man has already taken place in Jesus Christ, and only awaits the confirmation of our action.[2] The first affirmation which the Christian community makes about man's ethical situation is not that he must heroically take responsibility for himself, but that God has taken responsibility for man. It is only to this God that man is fully accountable in his thinking, willing and acting.[3]

Christian ethics cannot be tacked onto philosophical ethics like pinning a tail on a donkey. It must base its inquiry exclusively upon its own unique ground. Christian responsibility is not to be prematurely regarded as a particular instance of human responsibility in general.

The definition of "appropriate action" is already once-for-all decided and determined in the appropriate action of God. God's action, the right and appropriate action, is witnessed to in the proclamation concerning Jesus Christ. Here we see the appropriate action defined as that which gives itself in love and grace. Thus "to become obedient," "to act appropriately," "to realize the good," never means anything other than this: to become obedient to the revelation of the grace of God—to live as a man who has met with the grace of God in Jesus Christ.[4]

When we raise the question in the Christian community concerning what we ought to do, Barth says, we must ever raise the prior question of what God has done in Christ. In him the realization of the good is already a beheld "event." [5] In Christ the appropriate action of man is so completely realized that we, on our side, have only to endorse or confirm this event in our daily actions. Such a confirmation, however, is the full task of the Christian life.

De Facto Accountability. *All* men participate *de iure* (by juridical verdict) in the obedience of Christ. Whether men know it or acknowledge it, or order their lives in terms of it, Barth declares, God has taken responsibility for their lives in Jesus Christ. He is always already obedient in the place of all men.

Not all men participate *de facto* (in fact), however, in the obedience of Jesus Christ. By this Barth means we "on our side" often do not recognize and acknowledge the efficacy and reality of Christ's obedience for us. It is as if a verdict had been rendered in our favor, but we have either not heard about it or not believed that it was true for us. Christian existence is distinguished from all other ways of partial human existence in that it proceeds on the basis that God's verdict has been rendered in our favor and that it exerts legitimate authority over our lives. In short, the Christian participates *de facto* in the authentic human obedience in which all men participate *de iure*.[6]

[45]

Barth does not suggest that all men are given the *possibility* of participating in the obedience of Jesus Christ, and that only some men actualize this possibility. Rather, he says that all men participate in the *actuality* of the authentic obedience of Jesus Christ *de iure*. Their participation is a juridical participation, existing not by their own choice but by the choice of God. God's choice, however, may become our own, in which case our participation in true obedience is *de facto* and not merely *de iure*.[7]

Although all men exist under the new determination of God's grace *de iure*, God's determination only becomes from time to time man's self-determination when man's decisions *correspond* to the decisive activity of grace. But, Barth insists, the initiative of God must never be reduced to a "mere possibility" for men to actualize, but, rather, it stands as an already accomplished reality.[8]

Barth's main objection to Calvin's doctrine of election is that Calvin found no place for the universal relevance of the obedience of Christ for *all* men. The Christ of Calvin's *Institutes* did not die for the reprobate, and thus Christ's obedience has only limited, not universal, significance for all.

In answer to the question "What ought men to do?" Barth insists that we go back again in all strictness to the *content* of the gospel, which declares that Jesus Christ has fulfilled the law in our place. The law, or God's demand, points not merely to itself, but to God's grace. The only obligation (the law) for the Christian is to respond to the claim of grace.

All of the situational commands which are taken seriously in the Christian community witness finally to Jesus' fulfilling of these commands. Thus *the command in all the commands* is the *gospel*. The hearer is called to shape his action in the light of the action of God as witnessed to in the gospel. The formula which Barth uses to capture this relationship is that Jesus Christ is the form (*Form*) which requires our conformity (*Konformität*).[9]

Human Self-Determination under the Divine Predetermina-

[46]

tion. The obedience of Jesus Christ constitutes the divine pre-determination of authentic responsiveness in man. But the proclamation of God's election, Barth says, always raises the question of a corresponding human self-determination. The election of God calls for and enables a fitting response!

As we have seen, the church's inquiry into Christian ethics is not presuppositionless. It operates out of the acknowledged presupposition that God has chosen to take responsibility for man. But this proclamation of God's choice confronts man with the question of *how* he shall answer it; "*how* he shall exist under this determination; who he as such shall be thus determined, and *what* he as such shall do." [10]

"Human existence means human self-determination," [11] Barth writes. Man would not be man if he were a mechanism in the hands of God. Man is a self-determining being, although his self-determination exists in the context of other determinations.

Barth affirms the existentialist dictum that man *exists* in his deciding and acting. The same is true for Christian existence as well. The man who understands himself as subject to the gracious election of God still "understands himself as one who exists in his action and in his self-determination." [12] But while still being fully self-determined, the obedient man understands himself as existing simultaneously under the *determination of God.* Barth sees no contradiction whatsoever in the affirmation that man exists in his deciding and self-determining, and yet at the same time exists totally under the determination of the Word of God. We might formulate Barth's idea of simultaneous determination as follows: *Man's obedience to God is always a total self-determination under the total determination of God's summons.*[13]

How can it be maintained that man determines himself in the very act of his being determined by the command of God? In answering this, Barth operates on the same dialectic which may be found in Kant, although without the rationalistic presuppositions: Since man is a self-determining being, he can determine himself to be under the command of another. There is nothing logically inconsistent about deciding to will the decision of another. This is precisely the meaning of the obedience of faith: to determine oneself under the predetermination of the grace of God. Since God has decided about man, man can now decide about himself. One can choose to be the man God has chosen him to be.[14]

Barth categorically denies that man is a *mechanism* in the hands of God in the situation of obedience to God. He does say that God preshapes the will of the faithful man through his gracious claim. But he does not say that man's will is bound in this predetermination. It is a liberating verdict which God has rendered upon man. "Without taking away from men their freedom, their earthly substance, their humanity, without losing the human subject or making his action a mechanical occurrence, God is the subject from whom the human action must acquire its new, true name." [15]

The Embodiment of the Divine Claim. The command of God is known in its concrete form in Jesus Christ. Jesus embodies the divine decision concerning man. It is he who calls man to determine himself in accord with the predetermination of God. Man's will is "set in motion" [16] by Jesus Christ toward freedom for God, and therefore obedience to God.

Barth does not consider Jesus Christ as the mere vessel or shell of the command of God. It is not as if we open a husk in order to reach the content of the claim and then throw away the husk. Any moral claim which is not in some sense included in the claim of grace that is embodied in Jesus is regarded by Barth as something other than the claim of God. It is in Jesus Christ that men are discovered by "the God in whom they may truly believe." It is He who has shown himself to be "for us." Only such a trustable One can claim our total responsiveness.

Thus accountability to God is understood in the last analysis as accountability to the event of God's self-disclosure. The command of God is an event (Jesus Christ) just as the revelation of God is an event. God is one who commands in his activity, not in nonhistorical "ideas" or abstract "oughts." The event is not exclusively a past event, but on the contrary, a "constantly happening event." The Word of God in Jesus Christ is both an historical and an end-time (eschatological) event, grounded in a particular history and yet contemporaneous with every moment of our history.[17]

The Requirement Implicit in God's Electing Love. Man's ethical task is not merely in a general sense to "become responsible," but to learn what it means to affirm that God has made himself responsible for man. Included within the message that God has made himself responsible for man is the demand that man be responsible, or responsive to, God's decisive action.

Thus the predetermination or election of God lays upon man the requirement that he determine himself in terms of it. Election itself demands that it be understood as God's demand directed to man.[18] Yet if the question of *man's own answer* is never raised, Barth thinks that the Word of God has not been heard. Election is the sun, and obedience is its shining, says Barth—who can separate the two?

B. The Basis of the Divine Claim

The Sovereignty of God. We can only speak of the Word of God meaningfully when we acknowledge and celebrate its sovereignty and rightful authority. The news that God is for us always signifies the *arrest* of man in his self-assertiveness, as if it were the serving of a warrant upon him that he is not his own but is God's, and must come under a new Lordship.

Insofar as the address of God is heard, man understands God not as one power among others, but as the one and only power. If man knows nothing of this singular power, he only testifies that he knows nothing of the Word of God, to whom true Lordship belongs. Man knows God only as he is acquainted with this absolutely unique power. When man stands face to face with this one and only power, he stands "in the decision between the obedience which is due and the groundless inconceivability of disobedience." [19]

Not Might as Might. The basis of God's claim, however, is not "sheer might." Man is not coerced into accountability to God simply because it is inevitable that he submit to such might. Although God actually is this one and only power who is over and in all things, Barth says, this is *not* the ground of God's claim to our human obedience or of our obedience to his claim.

In fact, man stands radically *free* in the face of "might as might." [20] If the basis of God's claim is nothing other than sheer might, then man owes it no obedience. Man may be annihilated by it, but even the most overpowering might as such is not able to compel free man to obey it. For man is free in the face of power as such, and stands over against it as a self-determining creature. Man fulfills his preordination to freedom, according to Barth, by maintaining his freedom over against sheer might. Man is distinguished from the falling stone by freedom. But true freedom is that in which man determines himself in response to and for God through the neighbor.

Furthermore, the basis of God's claim, which calls forth radical accountability, is neither that God "is the essence of the good," nor my selection of God as my highest good, nor is it that he is the One who suffices all my needs. Within any of these frameworks, there can be no compelling basis for full accountability, since in each case the criterion finally lies within man rather than God. If the basis for responsibility to God consists finally in the fact that man on his side can choose God, then in this relationship there can be a divine claim only on the basis of "the claim which man has first placed upon God's election of him." [21]

If man must choose that there be a divine claim before the divine claim is established, this is a most precarious basis for ethics. Man could in that case today select God as his highest good, and tomorrow select a wholly different good.

Neither does the basis for total accountability to God lie in man's *faith*. Certainly there exists a circle of knowing, God and faith, faith and God, in which God is known in relation to man and man is known in relation to God. But this circle neither begins nor ends with the faith of man, Barth argues. The divine command is heard within this circle, but it never allows itself to be taken captive in the circle, as though the legitimacy of the command were in some sense finally dependent upon man's affirmation of it.

The God in Whom We May Have Faith. The only ground of the divine claim is that *the God who claims us for obedience is the God in whom we may have faith* (*der Gott, an den wir glauben dürfen*).[22] He has the right to claim us since he has shown himself to be the God who is *for us*. The basis of obedience to God is not that God is powerful, or our highest good, or the end of all our strivings, although he is all of these. It is rather that "he has given Himself to us!"[23] He has declared and shown himself to be, in the fullness of his deity, for us, and as such he is the One upon whom we may rely. Thus, the gospel, and nothing else, is the ground of our obedience. It is only *this* God, who is unmistakably for us, whom we can obey with all confidence.

Why should men obey God, therefore, and by what right does God claim man? The church offers no answer to this question except "that God is gracious to us in Jesus Christ." He claims us only on the ground that he has become one of us, and that we do not live out our human existence alone, but with him. In this Word lies "the validity of his command, and the nothingness of all other commands."[24] God's claim is not a second thing which belongs alongside his grace, but, rather, it is the claim which is addressed to man in and with grace itself.

To know God's grace is to know his Lordship. Mere knowledge of God's power can never compel man's fullest obedience, but knowledge of his grace does. It is therefore only in his grace in Jesus Christ that God comes to man as "the Almighty, as the good in person, as the One without whom there is no satisfaction." [25]

Genuine obedience is therefore never a matter of subjection to a self-legislated rule, since it is always a matter of free self-determination. Authentic freedom lives in response to the freedom of God.

C. Gospel and Law

Barth was convinced, along with Luther, that no single question is so fundamental to the Christian life as that of the relationship of gospel to law. It is evident that current political issues are deeply concerned with the function of the law, legalism, and licentiousness. In discussions of sexual ethics, the morality of war and revolution, and the ethics of police administration, the legitimacy of law is a fundamental, unavoidable question of our time. Unfortunately, the Christian community has not penetrated to the depths of this discussion with its own special wisdom concerning the gospel and its relation to the law. It is in this context that we turn to Barth's formulation of the relation of gospel and law, not only as a unique statement in the history of Christian ethics, but as one which speaks significantly to our current historical situation.

Law as the Form of the Gospel. The traditional order is first to speak of the law (what God demands of us or whatever moral requirements we feel upon ourselves) and only then to speak of the gospel as an answer to the problems created by the law. This is where Barth has made a remarkable contribution in his famous statement at Barmen in 1935 on "Gospel and Law," and later in volume II/2 of *Church Dogmatics*, where he turns the sequence around and argues that *we can only speak of the law in the context of the gospel.* Christian

aith does not call man to obedience to the law *per se*, just as
aw, but, rather, it sees law as enclosed in grace, as illuminated
oy the freedom of God for man. "The law would not be the
aw if it were not hidden and enclosed in the ark of covenant." [26]

God's Word always addresses man as grace, which means
hat it is free, nonobligatory divine goodness. The gospel has
grace as its particular content. Christian ethics, says Barth,
never refers to man's obligation to any law *per se*, but only to
he demand which is implicit in grace. The law is therefore
"relative to the gospel."

God's grace and God's command must be distinguished, but
hey cannot be separated. If we fail to distinguish them, or if
ve separate them completely, we do violence to the biblical
vitness. We can no longer speak of law, and only then separately of gospel, as if law were next to or outside the gospel.
t is in Jesus Christ that the proper relation of gospel and law
s made clear, since here we see the one who *is* grace, and yet
vho has kept the law. He is both the content of the gospel and
he fulfillment of the law. He is "the criterion by which we
have to measure all of our self-made concepts of laws and
norms." [27] Every command in the biblical witness is regarded
as having been already fulfilled in Jesus Christ.

The comprehensive formulation of the relation of gospel
and law which Barth sets forth is: *Law is the form of the
gospel.* The content of the gospel is grace, but the content demands a form. This form is the demand which grace lays upon
men. This is simply to say that "grace means . . . requirement and claim upon man." [28]

Exodus and Law. Throughout the biblical witness, legisla-
ion follows event. "Openly or secretly (but, as a rule, openly),
ts imperatives stand on its indicative." [29] Barth quotes Deuter-
onomy 6:20–21: "When your son asks you in time to come,
What is the meaning of the testimonies and the statutes and
he ordinances which the Lord our God has commanded
you?' then you shall say to your son, 'We were Pharaoh's

[53]

slaves in Egypt; and the Lord brought us out of Egypt with mighty hand. . . .'"

Always in the background, standing behind and supportin all Old Testament legislation, is this proclamation of delivei ance. Obedience never appears as an activity which in som way *precedes* the delivering occurrence, nor does it occur a that which merely stands alongside grace. Rather, the deman for obedience is always "the form, the *Gestalt*, the garment o grace." [30] So, just as obedience is never proclaimed in the ab stract, apart from grace, in the same way grace is never con sidered in the abstract, apart from the demand for obedience

In the biblical witness, there is no abstract rule of cultus "no abstract legal norm, no abstract moral law," [31] as if sucl rules, norms and laws could be separated from the commu nity's theological self-understanding. Everything which Israe is commanded to do in the law is merely an imperative transla tion of what Israel *is* by God's grace.

The command of God, in the New Testament, does no have materially or objectively new content over against Olc Testament law. Jesus is the new thing about the new law. He is the promised One for whom the law was first given to Israel In the light of his fulfillment of the law and all the promise of Israel, the New Testament sees all Old Testament legisla tion in a new light.

The law is in the gospel, and the gospel encloses the law Barth symbolizes this relationship by using an analogy of the ark of the covenant enclosing the tablets from Sinai. The tablets of law were carried *in* the ark, and the ark was the bearer of the tablets. The distinction between gospel and law cannot therefore mean a distinction between more and less or between better and worse. They are as different from eacl other as form and content, yet they are perfectly comple mentary.

God Himself as Doer of the Law. The law is valid because God himself is the doer of the law.[32] The uniqueness of the church's conception of responsibility hinges on this point, ac ording to Barth. The authenticity of the divine claim is established not by man's affirmation of the claim, but by the deed and decision of God himself, who himself rendered the obedience he demands in the ministry of Jesus Christ. "He is the God who has called man by Himself becoming man and as such not only demanding obedience, but performing it. He has spoken of the good by doing it." [33]

It is in his own obedience that God has established the right of his claim upon man. And this claim consists in nothing other than that man receive the good news that God has been obedient in our place.

Toward an Ethic of Celebration. It is now appropriate to ask: What is the relevance of all this? In honest and straightforward language, what might this mean for us?

In Barth we see the beginnings of an exciting new "ethic of celebration." We are called to affirm our humanity, since our humanity has been affirmed by God. We are called to take responsibility for our lives in the light of the proclamation that God himself has taken responsibility for us. We are called to share our lives with our neighbors, even as God himself has shared his life with us.

Barth is proposing a revolution in ethical reflection. Instead of merely asking, "What ought we to do?" he is calling us to ask, "What has God done to revolutionize our understanding of what we ought to do, and are being freed to do in response?" Instead of asking merely, "What is the good?" in an abstract sense, he is calling us to ask, "How is God's goodness meeting us in such a way as to revolutionize all our human norms of goodness?"

The essential proposal of this book is that *Barth's ethic is promising because it is an ethic of freedom.* Although we will have much more to say later about the redefinition of freedom, the central thrust of Barth's ethic is already before us: Man is being called to be free, to be himself before God, in response to the freedom of God for him. There is no claim of God except the claim implicit in the good news that God is for us.

[55]

There is no requirement of God apart from the liberating claim that addresses us in the Christ event. The most profound moral claim upon man is not society's law or the competing claims of conscience, but the constraining power of God's redemptive love which calls man to love in response to it. It is in radical responsiveness to the trustworthiness of God that genuine human freedom is actualizable. In this sense the Christian life is fundamentally a life of celebration—a celebration of a humanity which God himself has shared, a celebration of our own being as honored by God's being with us and for us, a celebration of free human self-determination under the shaping power of the freedom of God for man.

Barth's ethic is a consistent reversal of our puritanisms which have always put law before gospel (i.e., which have always pretended to make us qualify for God's goodness on the basis of our good deeds). The reversal consists in the fact that the good news of God's reconciling action is the axiomatic beginning (not merely the last chapter) of the Christian understanding of moral requirement.

Why is this so relevant? Because the emerging generation is fed up with the legalisms of the parent generation, and is struggling for a new conception of moral responsibility based upon freedom, love and honest accountability to each other. It is ready (legitimately, I think) to speak some word about the liberation of man. Admittedly there may be some antinomian temptations in Barth's conception of the law as an implication of grace, and of command as permission. I do not suggest that this ethic is without its difficulties and problems. Anyone who places such consistent emphasis upon God's action as the basis of our responsive action is tempted from time to time to fall into an innocuous quietism or otherworldly passivity (which Marx so rightly criticized). But Barth has seen these temptations as keenly as his critics and has tried to guard against his views being misinterpreted in this direction.

At least it is clear that the emerging generation is hungering for some more profound understanding of Christian freedom than sheer brow-beating, breast-beating legalism has provided. An ethic which focuses on the freedom of man in constant awareness of the freedom of God may surely be made more plausible to the emerging generation, and is much more in tune with the action today, than are the duller ethical perspectives which begin with the impossible Oughts that man feels bulging out every side of his superego, ripping the seams of his personhood with idealized and weighty self-addressed imperatives. It is against this sort of bind that Barth's ethic struggles, seeking to liberate man into a life style of responsive freedom.

III.

The Command of God:
A Situation Ethic?

Having established his basic theological vantage point, we will now begin an exposition of Barth's understanding of the *command* of God, and of the relation of *freedom and obedience*. Throughout this discussion we will be concerned with the relation between *permission and obligation*, "may" and "ought." This dialectic is crucial in Barth's ethic since, in his view, freedom for God and obedience to God mean the same thing. In setting forth this dialectic, we will clarify how the command lays hold of man's will and determines him to good activity, enabling him to overcome the conflict of obligations through "simple obedience" to the command.

The basic issues: How does permission constitute a command? How does Barth avoid legalism in his view of the command of God? What is the nature of a command? In what sense is man free when the command determines his will?

A. Simple Sensitivity

The Unique Presupposition of Christian Ethics. The electing grace of God in Jesus Christ has been secured as the point of departure for every question and answer concerning man's responsibility. This presupposition must never be surpassed, undone, negated or amended. When one begins, for example, with a fixed preconception of "the idea of a command," as might be determined by some general moral philosophy, the distinctly Christian beginning point has already been put aside. If we begin with a general concept of ethics and inquire abstractly into "the good," "value," or "obligation," seeking a standard by which human action may be measured as responsible or irresponsible, we have already "surpassed," and therefore never understood, the unique presupposition of Christian ethics.[1]

The Christian ethic does not emerge on the basis of the assumption that the command of God is *not* known to man, and that man must somehow discover it. It does not begin with man asking himself what he ought to do, or in what his authentic life consists, but, rather, with acknowledgment or attestation that the command of God is already once for all made *clear*. Christian ethical inquiry takes place within the circle of the church's special witness, and moves from its own unique presupposition, Emmanuel (God with us), taking the form of self-clarification of that presupposition.[2] Thus the church's inquiry into responsibility to God begins by placing in question all ordinary conceptions of responsibility, and by proclaiming the news of God's decision to take responsibility for man. The Christian community has nothing to gain by hiding this central presupposition or pretending it is unimportant.[3]

Just as Barth's theology determines his ethics, likewise his ethics impinges powerfully upon every aspect of dogmatics. Dogmatics itself is an act of obedience, an act in which the inquirer acknowledges that he is not the master of the inquiry, but that the inquiry would be groundless were it not for self-disclosing divine grace.

The witness of the church is likewise an act of obedience. It is nothing more than the "answer" which the church makes to the Word of God. It is a *human* answer, Barth emphasizes, something that *man* does, with limited human language, upon hearing this Word. But it is also, from time to time, God's own Word, and not merely a human word, when God chooses to make his Word known in human language. Church proclamation is an act of obedience insofar as it acts upon the promise of the divine Word becoming a human word, and intends and hopes to be the Word of God, albeit in human language.[4]

Barth forewarns, however, that it is quite beyond man's direct control as to whether or not this human word becomes an authentic act of proclamation. Man does not stand in a position to manipulate the command of God. The church's obedience in fact consists in its acknowledgment that its proclamation as such is never God's Word unless and until God chooses to make it his own.

The Nature of a Command. Barth constructs a remarkable argument designed to reconceive the very notion of a command. To obey a command does not mean, according to Barth, that one first examines it and becomes convinced that it is good, and only then affirms it. Rather, the command tells us what is good. For example, the command tells us we ought to love our neighbor. If we first sought to become entirely convinced that we should love our neighbor and only then acted on the basis of our being fully convinced, then we would never love our neighbor at all. If we are correctly to understand the meaning of the command *as command*, then we approach it not by trying to explain it, but by the doing of it. In short, knowing of God's command is found only in the keeping of it.[5]

It is only when the moral claim upon man is grounded in such a way that man cannot take up an attitude of reserve toward it, that it can be genuine ground for full and free obedience. If man can still appeal to his own spurious freedom, authority or self-will over against the demand, then the command cannot be God's command. If a command is truly to appeal to the total man and claim his complete responsiveness, it must not merely *require* something of man, but it must also *enable man to fulfill the requirement.*[6]

[60]

The only claim, therefore, which can claim man's total obedience is the claim of God's grace, the claim of one who is himself obedient in our place. Only this claim has power and authority to deprive man of recourse to his own self-righteousness. All other commands give man some ground upon which to make a counterclaim. But since God's claim comes to man in the form of grace, it disarms man and makes all counterclaims groundless.[7]

From this point, Barth comes to the remarkable conclusion that *any word which can be obeyed or disobeyed upon hearing it, is not God's Word.* "To hear the Word of God means, since it is the Word of the Lord, to obey the Word of God."[8] Barth regards it as self-deception to think that one can disobey the command of God, once it is truly heard.

The Clarity of the Word of God. Barth sharply rejects that ethic which would allow man to make his own private interpretation of the meaning of God's command. He vigorously champions Bonhoeffer's treatment of "simple obedience" (*einfältiger Gehorsam*), which, he says, is "easily the best that has been written on this subject." Simple obedience is "that obedience in which a man just does what is commanded him, no more and no less, and nothing other than just that."[9] When man simply obeys, he does what he is asked to do, "literally and exactly."

But when man seeks to make his own special interpretation of the command, doing what he thinks is *implicit* in the command, rather than merely doing what it explicitly commands, he never "simply obeys" the command. The man who does not think he needs to do just what the command *explicitly* situationally summons him to do, Barth says, has never yet taken the command seriously. He who searches for the "true sense" of the command never is "simply obedient" to it. The interpreter of the command is always tempted to impose his own counterclaim upon the command, and thus rejects the command *as a command.*

In line with Bultmann and Kant, Barth argues that the

[61]

command of God is always clear and unambiguous, in the sense that the address of the situation is fully concrete, even though we may fail to respond to its correctness. It never comes to man in such a way that the man himself is given any room for consideration of why and how he may best follow the command given, or interpret it correctly. The command of God always presents man with a concrete and particular thing to do. Obedience to God is never a general attitude, he says, but always a concrete and particular action.

"Simple sensitivity" (to others, to reality, to God's here-and-now claim) may be a better English rendering of "simple obedience." Sensitivity training, which seeks to make one more aware of the claim of the concrete situation in which one exists, is profoundly akin to this situational ethic.

The Command and the Situation. It is on this basis that Barth rejects the distinction between "what is commanded" and "what the command *means* in this situation." [10] The claim of grace always has content only in its explicit situational form. The hearer of the command of God is not called to distinguish between its implicit content and its explicit form. There is no abstract, implicit responsibility, but only explicit, concrete, situational sensitivity.

If so, then man cannot "store up" patterns or habits of obedient activity for future use. This constitutes a rejection of a traditional ethic of virtue, with its dependence on the notion of *habitus*. The Christian ethic does not derive concrete action from some remote supply of implicit commands which are then applied to particular situations. Content (situational action) and form (the command) are inseparable.

Nor is obedience to the command of God taking place when one prudently postpones a full inward and outward rendering of obedience until he finds a favorable psychological, historical, economic or political situation for it. Man does not have to create a "favorable situation" for obedience to God. The creative action of God itself creates the situation, Barth writes, and all the conditions of the situation in which man has to obey.

Is Simple Obedience Legalistic? Discursive, casuistic, dialectical obedience which endlessly memorializes the command but never acts upon it is at heart legalistic, Barth charges, even though it often takes the role of championing antilegalism. He argues that simple obedience is not legalistic, even though it obeys the situational demand literally and exactly, for in simple obedience, action is spontaneous, not casuistic or deliberative. In simple responsiveness, *what* is required is determined not by man but by the commanding situation! Barth's basic pattern is not formally different from that which we find in Kant, in which obedience is objectively under the determination of the moral law, and subjectively determined by respect for it.

There is a sense of immediacy and situationality, however, in Barth, which is much more akin to the existentialist tradition than to Kant. Obedience to the claim of grace can only be rendered "immediately and in the present moment." [11] He who is obeying is not merely prepared or ready to leap, but, rather, he is already leaping.

The Synoptic Gospels' Prototype. Barth frequently turns to the synoptic narratives of the call of the disciples in elucidating his ethic of responsiveness. It is not that we are to imitate their responsiveness, but be responsive to the One to whom they are responsive. The contemporary disciple is called to radical responsiveness without discussion or reserve, without endless appraisal of other possibilities, and without waiting for a favorable situation in which to respond, just as the disciples unreservedly followed the call of the messianic servant.

We may copy every "rule" which Jesus demanded of his disciples and yet completely fail to follow *him* obediently. In fact it would be just another form of disobedience if we were content merely to codify the commands he gave the Twelve and regard them as his command for us, rather than follow

[63]

him as did the disciples. The disciples did not first of all choose to follow Jesus; rather, he chose them and they responded by answering his call. Just as Jesus' call was a direct and personal call to the particular disciple in his special situation, so it is with the contemporary disciple in his current context.

The Messianic Summons. The basic form of the call to discipleship is: "Follow me!" [12] The only way to respond affirmatively to the messianic command is to lay aside whatever one is doing, prior to it, and follow. The man who first wanted to bid farewell to those in his house, and *then* be obedient to the messianic summons, was not responsive because he sought to lay down a condition of his own in answer to the demand. Since the command is unconditionally commanded, it cannot be conditionally obeyed. All it requires is "simple obedience."

The question whether or not one is *"really"* obedient to the command of God is "idle speculation," since it so readily focuses on man's judgment and determination, rather than on the objective claim of the situation in which God addresses man. "It is up to God and not to us to judge whether our hearing is genuine hearing and our obedience genuine obedience." [13]

Throughout our whole discussion of Barth it has been apparent that faith and obedience stand in a close relationship. Now is the time to make that relationship explicit.

What does the command of God direct us to do? Summarily: "We ought to have faith in Jesus Christ." To *act* in conformity with God's grace is to *attest* God's grace in one's action. To *conform* to God's demand is to *recognize* God's demand in one's action. To obey God is to *accept it as right* that God's action is good, and that the only goodness of our action is its conformity with God's action. [14]

What sort of doing and obeying does Barth propose for us? Accept, believe, attest, witness, recognize! In emphasizing the confessionalist character of action, as a demonstration of something, Barth resembles Schleiermacher, for whom the most important aspect of Christian ethics was representative or demonstrative action.[15] There is nothing in the New Testament narratives to indicate that the disciples first believed, and then as a second decision, decided to obey and follow. Obedience does not begin after faith, but has its beginning within the decision of faith. For "as obedience without faith is not obedience, so faith without obedience is not faith." [16]

The summons to faith and obedience, or as Paul expresses it, *upakoe pisteos,* the obedience of faith, always calls man to make a complete break with whatever he may have been following, and to make a wholly new beginning. The call to discipleship always involves "a turn of 180 degrees" in which one turns one's back upon the old self and turns toward the new man. Christian obedience is not basically a program, an ideal or a law, but an answer one makes to the One who issues the command to discipleship. Thus faith and obedience are inseparable moments of the one occurrence: man's response to the call to discipleship, man's answer to the Word and command of God.

B. Obedience as Permission

The Unexpected Equation. To be free means to be under the command of God and to allow the command to determine one's action, rather than to be free spuriously to say Yes or No to the command. Man's authentic freedom is freedom for God, and thus obedience. It is not the capacity for either obedience or disobedience. Fundamentally, Barth's position is not unlike that of Kant, who defined freedom as the determination of the will by the moral law. Kant regarded the free will not as the ability to say Yes or No to the moral law, but as that will which is wholly independent of all inclinations and passions and emotive interpretations, and thus under the exclusive determination of the moral law of reason.

[65]

The faithful man does not stand as Hercules at the cross-roads, in the position of choosing good or evil, as if man's good consisted in his own choice of the good. "No, it is in that he is elected by God's grace that the good is done. As one who is chosen, quite apart from any choice of his own between good and evil, he concerns himself only with obedience. He does not covet being good of and for himself. Therefore in all his acts he is subject only to the will and command of God who alone is good." [17]

The Christian ethic deals with man, not merely as he chooses himself (Martin Heidegger, Jean-Paul Sartre), but as God has chosen him to be, viz., made righteous in Jesus Christ. The obedient man no longer even attempts to locate the good within his own will, but in all his activity acknowledges God's good choice as *his* good.

This is the heart of Barth's understanding of freedom. Essentially man's freedom consists in his being elected by God to be free for God, free for life and free for his neighbor. To be obedient to God means to be free to be a true man, as God has chosen man to be.

The free man never acts as if he himself had to decide autonomously, by himself, concerning the nature of the moral good, for the good is not something for man first of all to *do*, but for him to acknowledge as already having been done.

The Single Possibility. Christian obedience consists in the *use* of the freedom for which Christ has set man free, not the use of the so-called freedom of the "old man" to obey or disobey. The true issue of obedience and disobedience lies in whether or not man embraces or neglects the freedom for which Christ has set him free. Disobedience does not consist in freedom being *misused*, since true freedom for God, for self and for neighbor *cannot* be misused. It can only be put to use or nonuse.[18] Disobedience consists simply in the neglect, ignorance and disregard of true human freedom.

So Barth understands that in obedience to God there is but *one* possibility, whereas in all other idolatrous loyalties there are *many possibilities*. The single possibility of Christian obedience is that freedom to *be* who one *is*, under the permission of grace, as a new creature.

Obedience to God is a very definite willing, acting and thinking out of this one possibility, rather than a constantly ambiguous choosing between alternatives. The crux of man's disobedience is his acting as though his freedom could have some other beginning than that which is continually being established by the occurring love of God. It is tragically true that although man is in fact being liberated by God's gracious decision, he nevertheless absurdly wills, acts and thinks as if he were not in truth free.

In his doctrine of sanctification, Barth says that the Holy Spirit, who instructs man in the life of obedience, continually lays before man the one possibility of his new creaturehood in Christ, helping him to distinguish between the new and the old presuppositions for action. The Holy Spirit champions man's freedom against the many possibilities of spurious self-will.[19]

The tragic character of disobedience lies in the fact that man rejects the gift of his own true freedom. Sin is never anything other than man's insistence that he can be independent of grace and make his own way through the maze of his own goods and evils. Sin is never, in Barth's view, a violation of an abstract legal relationship, but always a concrete rejection of grace amid the incredible desire to live as an alien far away from one's true home.[20]

Barth rejects the notion that the possibility of sin (*posse peccare*) was given to man's nature or was a part of his created being, and that such was the option exercised in the fall. The only freedom for which man is created is exclusively a freedom *for God*. The freedom to obey or disobey was precisely the kind of freedom that is denied by God's command.

Freedom is not room for movement at the edge of an abyss. It is freedom *for responsiveness*, and freedom *from* irresponsiveness to grace. It is not some sort of space between obedience and disobedience. God gives man freedom exclusively for the purpose of being truly obedient.[21]

The Special Form of the Command of God. It is from this special perspective that Barth surprisingly comes to the view that the distinguishing mark of the command of God is that it *commands man to be free.* Man is not free except in answer to God's command to be free. Man does not achieve authentic freedom as a sheer act of self-will. It is only in response to the claim of grace. In becoming obedient to God's command to be free, man simply becomes himself. He becomes who he is: a man free for God and for his neighbor.

This does not mean that man's decision now takes the place of God's decision. Rather, it means that man's activity is made free through correspondence with God's activity. Man remains creature before the Creator, but his creaturely activity is sanctified by the command to be who he is, i.e., a free creature. Man cannot exalt himself, but he is paradoxically exalted in his subordination to the command of God.[22]

The special form by which the command of God is distinguished from all other commands is *permission* (*Erlaubnis*), the offering of a very definite freedom. Because it is a command of grace, it takes the form of permission. No other command except the command of God presents itself to man in this special form, for only in this command does man know that the Commander is none other than the God in whom he may believe, the God who is infinitely *for* him.

To be sure, man stands under a plethora of commands in any given historical moment. Each of them in its own way claims to be ultimate and decisive. Each attacks and lays claim upon the will. Barth goes so far as to say that every object in the natural and historical world lays potential claim upon man and demands his consideration and attention. None of these claims in nature and history in itself constitutes the claim of God.

The distinguishing mark which differentiates the claim of grace from all these claims is its special form: permission. All other commands bind and restrict man. They are secretly suspicious of his freedom, assuming that if he were truly free he would misuse his liberty. "Such commands are essentially special pleadings, and consequently the denial of all possible permission." [23] They do not allow man to go his own way, but fill him with moral despair concerning his own freedom.

The Sabbath Command. Christian morality is concerned not so much that man *ought* to act in a certain way, but that he *may* act in a certain way. Barth uses the Sabbath command as an example of permission. This command at heart means: "You *may* take a day of rest," not, "You *ought to* take a day of rest." [24] Yet it remains a command, although all it establishes is a permission. Even in saying, "You *may*," it calls man to make use of this permission.

Barth sees a broad analogue for an ethic of freedom in the notion that the Sabbath command requires nothing but liberation. It asks man merely to be free from work.

Obedience to the command to take a day of rest consists essentially in acknowledging that God has taken up our cause in his own hands. To obey this command, therefore, means nothing other than faith. Although the Sabbath command refers to a particular day, Barth suggests that it is a parable of every day of human activity. [25]

The Enabling of Freedom. One of the most surprising facets of Barth's ethic of freedom is his conclusion that, in the last analysis, *the demand of God actually commands man to act on his own decision!* [26] In obedience to the command of God, man simply makes use of the permission given him by grace to become who he *is*, viz., a free, self-determining creature. The command of God sets man on his feet as a human being. It is not a "rule" set over against him. It is against him only insofar as he is against himself.

This is not to suggest that authentic human freedom is, in the last analysis, arbitrary self-assertiveness. The command of God sets itself against such arbitrary self-will, in order that man may be truly free. Even when the command meets man in the form "Thou shalt not!" it always sets him in a position to be free for God and the neighbor.

Situationally, the command of God may claim man by saying, "Leave this alone." For certain actions would merely be a perpetuation of the old life from which man has been set free. Thus the command says, in effect, "You *may* leave these things alone" because, before God, you are free from their spurious demand, exempt from the necessity of acting thus, and cut off from these negated possibilities.[27]

Barth is not suggesting that God confirms a permission that man gives himself. Rather, man confirms and makes use of the permission placed at his disposal by grace. Other permissions than the command of grace always finally come back to the self for their authority or source. The command of grace engages man at such close quarters that he is cut off from retreat upon himself.

Thus Barth argues that the command of God secures man's obedience in a wholly unique fashion: by setting man free. Only the command of grace demands and orders that man be free to be who he is, since only he could give such a command who has demonstrated himself to be one in whom man may infinitely trust.

The command of God is easily distinguished from man's appetites, desires and lusts, because it always has the form of permission rather than necessity. Man's desires always put him under necessity, as if they stood, as it were, over against man. The only necessity contained in the command of God is the permission which calls him to be who he is.[28]

C. The Shaping Power of the Command

The Determination of the Will. The claim of grace is such that it has power to constrain man to determine himself in terms of it. It has a kind of "teleological power," says Barth, to reach out aggressively and draw the existing individual toward responsiveness. The *telos* of the command is to make man free, and to dislodge the old purposes of the disobedient man made obsolete by the decision of God in Jesus Christ.

The command of God is not given to man in vain. It *finds* man, Barth declares, and provides his self-determining will with an impulse to obedience. The initiating impulse is the fundamental divine decision to create man anew. The teleological power of grace thus constrains and persuades man increasingly to become the partner of the gracious God of the covenant. "It determines man's actions to conformity and correspondence with God's action." [29] In this determination, man's action becomes a mirror or reflection of the prior action of God. Note, however, that although human action re-presents God's action, it remains (as a mirror) wholly different from God.

The command of God requires and permits that man's creaturely life, being, action, thought, words and works acquire this correspondence to God's own life. In so doing, man reflects the image of God. Such correspondence of the life of man to the life of God, the resurrection of the image of God in man, is not a mere possibility but an actuality in Jesus Christ.

The teleological power of the command is cause for rejoicing, since it aids the will in obeying. Barth speaks of the simplicity and lightness of the command of God. It asks one thing only of man: "that what we do, we should do as those who accept as right what God in his grace does for us." [30]

God does not demand more than man can perform. His demand sets in motion the will of man toward the performance of what is demanded. If the yoke of the moral requirement is too heavy to be borne, then one may be assured that it is not the divine requirement. If a claim asserts itself over man but does not carry with it "the refreshment of grace," then Barth regards that claim as being wholly distinct from the divine claim, since the divine claim has teleological power to enable its hearer to accomplish it.

Conflicting Obligations Overcome. The command of grace

summons man away from the alien and wretched realm of *the conflict of obligations*. The command of grace transforms the realm of many obligations into the realm of a single permission.

Man as sinner tries to set himself up as the judge and orderer of these many claims. He tries desperately to classify values and obligations and arrange them in an appropriate hierarchy. He longs to satisfy all their relative claims, as they seem legitimate, but since each of these obligations claims to be absolute, man finds it impossible to satisfy them absolutely. In this way he becomes a slave to the plethora of moral obligations.

The command of grace is *not* the sum of all legitimate demands, humanly speaking. Neither is it another command which is added to all of them. On the contrary, it is a command which relativizes, and, in a sense, "puts aside" all these commands which had claimed to be absolute. It claims man under the single simple permission that he ought to be the new and free creature whom God has decided that he shall be.[31]

Genesis 3 forms the basis for Barth's discussion of the way in which the command overcomes the conflict of obligations. The fall, as man's absurd disobedience, is symbolized as man's choice to eat of the tree of the knowledge of good and evil. The fall is understood as the beginning of conflicts of value. Man exalts himself in a spurious Godlikeness when he seeks himself to make the choice between good and evil, instead of remaining responsive in his original freedom for God. He finds himself anxiously thrust into the realm of the plethora of commands. He takes upon himself the anxiety-laden task of deciding which command is good and which is evil. Thus man is confronted on all sides by many commands and prohibitions, claims and counterclaims, cast in awesome contradiction with one another. Barth caricatures such a man: "His eyes are now open but only like those of a victim of insomnia. He now has to choose and decide and judge on all sides. He has to try to hew a track for himself through the unending primeval forest of claims." [32]

To play at being Creator and Lord is something which man cannot do quite successfully. Indeed, man's deepest ethical misery lies in the fact that he cannot satisfy all the claims which surround him, and in fact cannot really satisfy a single one of them, because each one aims at being supreme.

It is the teleological power of the command of God which relentlessly brings man back to his proper beginning point. It does not place man under a "higher" obligation, but puts man on his feet by calling him to be who he is.

The new point of departure is the new man created by God's decision, not the old man who has been "put off." The new man is *free* continually to begin again at the point of God's reconciliation. He is not given many possibilities, but only one actuality: his new creaturehood in Christ.[33]

D. Toward a New Ethic of Sensitivity

Again we come to ask, without evasions or self-deceptions, what all this means to us. What promise does it bear?

Ethical discussions today are plagued with élitist notions of ethical decision-making which assume that ordinary people are incapable of serious moral judgment, and that they must turn over their moral decisions to élite, expert decision-makers. In Christian ethics this appears in the notion that political ethics are too complex for ordinary folk to know anything about, and that only the experts are qualified to render adequate judgments. "Simple sensitivity" cuts right through that façade of expertise with the assertion that every man is concretely accountable in every moment. It calls every man to listen intently to the address of the Holy Spirit in the situation in which he exists. It assumes that the command of God is borne concretely and clearly within each unique context.

The situation itself is addressing you, the individual, concretely with what you are to do. It is now, and not some other time or some idealized situation, which calls you to "simple sensitivity" to the command of God. That command is not something you give yourself. That leads into absurd rationalizations and self-justifications. The command addresses you wholly through the context. It asks you to do something quite specific, to really *be* there, to swing with the situation, to answer it with your own imaginative response.

You cannot play games with the demand of God at this level of concreteness. If you really hear it, you are already in the process of answering it responsively with your total being and doing. Thus, so far as the situationality and clarity of the command of God is concerned, Barth's ethic of "simple sensitivity" is very similar to Bultmann's ethic of "radical obedience." The difference lies in their varied conceptions of authenticity: for Bultmann, authenticity is existentially defined with the emphasis upon an appropriate self-understanding; whereas for Barth, the authentic man is the covenant man who is known, finally, in Jesus Christ.

There is an influential movement in group psychotherapy and group dynamics today which is concerned with "sensitivity training." Through various tactile and verbal encounters and strategies, this approach seeks to help persons simply to learn to hear one another, empathize, feel another's feelings, be responsive to others' needs and claims. Barth's ethic is profoundly akin to this direction. Barth is simply saying: "Wake up! Be aware of the clear and concrete claim which is addressing you in the moment. It is not merely an abstract, legal or conceptual claim. It is God's own address asking for a concrete response. If you are really *in* the situation, with all your sensory and imaginative apparatus geared to it, then you will not find it possible to dodge its claim with your own well-constructed defenses and self-justifying rationalizations."

Admittedly, the strength of Barth's ethics is not in any sort of deliberative, calculative criteria for moral choice. If that is all that one is looking for under the heading of "ethics," then surely Barth will be a consistent disappointment. Although he does engage in some attempts at developing guidelines for responsible behavior in *Church Dogmatics*, III/4, on many issues such as suicide, birth control, abortion, conscientious objection, etc., this is not the real strength of his ethic. The real strength is in what might be called its "theologically interpreted radical contextuality." Barth is no ordinary contextualist, since he understands the "context" in an utterly fresh way. He is not saying merely that what man has to learn morally must be learned ever anew from the context in which he exists, although he is indeed saying that. More so he is placing the context itself in a revolutionary interpretive framework, viz., the history of the covenant God, as made known in the story of the people of Israel and the Christ event. It is with that memory, utilizing the full perceptual apparatus which emerges out of the Judeo-Christian tradition, that one comes to the situation and listens for its highly specific claim. That claim has total credibility because of its radical concreteness.

This need not imply that serious response to the claim of God involves no deliberation or reflection as to what to do about it. It certainly may involve the calculation of goals and deliberation on precedents and consequents in order to grasp what is to be done and to carry out some responsive action. But the command itself is not finally dependent upon our interpretations of it. The command is concretely and therefore unambiguously addressing us wherever we are, even though, due to our bugged and distorted perceptual mechanisms, we hear it ambiguously and unclearly.

The question may be raised whether or not Barth's ethic of simple obedience is mere slave morality which has been so rightly rejected by Nietzsche and others. Although Barth sometimes gives that impression, it surely is a misunderstanding. The difference is this: In slave morality, the commander stands wholly over against the slave without participating in his situation, as an alien to his suffering. In Barth's ethic of freedom, the one who commands in the situation is One who has made himself known as trustworthy by himself participating in our human condition. Thus we can trust ourselves to a serious engagement with the address of reality itself. We can trust that such an engagement will lead us into a fuller humanity. That is not slave morality. It is simple sensitivity to now, dancing with the rhythms of life, swinging with the situation.

IV.

Human Responsibility

The question that remains generally unanswered is that of the special character of our own human response to the command of God. We have spoken of the obedience of Jesus Christ in our place, and indicated that our actions are called to correspond to this predetermination of our authentic being. But it remains to be shown *how* man is called to respond to the claim of grace, or *what* he is called to do in his new creaturehood. In the ensuing pages we would like to press Barth as far as we can with the question concerning our *de facto* human (all-too-human) obedience, what it involves and in what it consists.

Therefore we shall begin with a study of "The True Man," stating the anthropological basis upon which Barth insists when speaking of "human obedience." Then having spoken of the being of the true man, we will be able to speak of his doing. And it is appropriate to ask, in this connection, about Barth's view of the role of the Holy Spirit in the responsible life, along with a number of other questions.

A. The True Man

Christological Anthropology. The only "man" of whom Barth will speak is "God's man." [1] He rejects the notion of an independent anthropology. He refuses to speak of man as such. Christian anthropology, in contrast to all other anthropologies, inquires exclusively into that human creatureliness which stands in covenant relation to God. We find Barth ready and willing to speak about man, but always only on the ground of the church's distinctive presuppositions.

Scientific inquiry into man's observable situation, such as phenomenological studies carried on by sociologists and psychologists, are in no sense the enemy of Christian proclamation and theology, and empirical studies do not constitute a threat to the church. But, Barth says, they have a different purpose, viz., seeing man as a phenomenon. They do not inquire into man's authentic being, or into God's decision concerning man.

Christian anthropology takes its exclusive beginning point in God's election of man to be his covenant partner. From this vantage point, Christian anthropology is interested to show not only man's authentic relationship to God, but also man in his "perversion and corruption, as sinner against his creaturely essence." [2] But even in man's perversion of his authentic created essence as covenant man, he does not and cannot destroy the covenant relation, since God is its initiator. Therefore, whether man thinks he lives within or without the covenant, he is nevertheless to be properly understood as a partner of the covenant. Since the covenant relation is fulfilled and only made clear in Jesus Christ, Barth regards the only adequate anthropology as a Christological anthropology, i.e., man must be seen never as prior to Christ, but as always already a participant in Christ.

In the final analysis, Jesus is the true man. That means: it is only in the man Jesus that we can see this covenant relation clarified. To be sure, we know ourselves to be abysmally different from him in many ways, but we may be assured that the creaturely being of Jesus and of ourselves is the same. The yawning gulf, however, between the man Jesus and men as they are is only the absurd and terrible fact of sin, man's affirmation of that which God has negated.

Actual Man. To understand what man is, we must see what he is before God. This is made clear in the man Jesus. God does not become less than God, and man does not become more than man in obedience of Jesus Christ. In his actions he determines himself under God's predetermination.

Barth rejects the notion that the sinful, proud, insensitive man may be considered as actual or real man. Actual man is seen in the man Jesus who was, in every decision, for God. His freedom consists in his freedom to decide for the covenant, not his "unfreedom" to be slothful and proud. Actual man is given permission, in the covenant relation, to be "for God." This constitutes both his freedom and obedience as well as his true essence. The destiny of the true man's freedom is to honor and serve God.

Consequently, Barth argues, to the great surprise of many of his hearers, that authentic freedom and obedience are not to be regarded as *possibilities* for man, but, rather, as *actualities* always already given to man. Many Christian ethical theorists, in contrast, write of freedom and obedience only in the framework of possibility. Bultmann, for instance, speaks of free obedience as the lost possibility of man as such, which becomes an actual possibility only when man is confronted by the deed of God. Barth, on the other hand, argues that as long as obedience to God is a mere empty human possibility which has to be seized and actualized by human thinking, willing and doing, then it is profoundly impossible. Obedience to God must be seen rather as a "fulfilled possibility! As actuality!" [3] in Jesus Christ, the true man.

The concept of a "humanity which is grounded in itself," Barth says, is illusory, and should not be taken seriously. The kerygma insists that "there is no humanity outside the humanity of Jesus Christ." [4] Barth thinks all non-Christological anthropologies are abstract, in the sense that they, in effect, abstract man out of the covenant relation.

Since Schleiermacher, theologians have sought to understand God through an analysis of man, attempting to move from anthropological to theological knowledge, Barth observes. This is a sequence which he believes to be defeated before it starts. Any inquiry into human responsibility which begins with the human self cannot end with knowledge of God's command. The imperatives which man addresses to himself cannot amount to the command of God. Only a covenantal perspective can render adequate self-knowledge. "For there is no good which is not obedience to God's command. And there is no obedience to God's command which is not the obedience of Jesus Christ." [5]

Being and Doing. Barth speaks of Christian existence as both a being and a doing. Faith and obedience are related as being and doing are related. Justification and sanctification are related as faith and obedience are related. And yet in each case, both terms form a single reality, Christian existence.

The new being of man is called forth by God's decision in Jesus Christ. Such is the true man, freely and obediently living under the predetermination of this divine decision as a new subject, *peccator justus,* a justified sinner.

The new being of man does not subsist of itself. It lives only out of the divine election. And it always exists in *action,* i.e., man's being is not a static quality, but constantly manifesting itself in acting and deciding. The doing of the new man always eventuates out of his being. "A special doing is made unavoidable by one's being. One cannot suppress or conceal or keep to himself what he *is.*" [6] The Word of God summons man to be who he is through his doing.

Barth in this way affirms the existentialist dictum that "it is as he acts that man exists as a person." [7] The ethical question ordinarily concerns the rightness, worth or goodness of man's activity. Consequently if the ethical question is to be answered, Barth says, man himself must in some way *be* the answer. It is precisely of *man himself* that the Christian proclamation speaks, in the message that man himself is made anew in Jesus Christ.

The true man does not give, but *is* the answer to the question of human responsibility. What is the proper action? It is that which has taken place in Jesus Christ. What is the good and the valuable? It is that which exists in Jesus Christ. He

[80]

is the concrete fulfillment of God's command. He is the fully human answer to the ethical question.[8]

B. The Inclusion of Human Action
within the Action of God

The New Man. In order to speak to the question of human *action*, Barth has forced us to raise the question of man's *being*, the being of the new man in Jesus Christ. We cannot now retreat to a consideration of the action of the old man, who from God's point of view has no legitimized existence in the created order. If we are to ask properly the question of human action, we must speak of man as he actually is, as one whom, according to the church's witness, God has chosen for covenant partnership in Jesus Christ.

Barth's reader is repeatedly warned that he should no longer attempt to view human action in abstraction from "revelation itself." The question which Barth's reader wants to put constantly to him, conversely, is whether he tends to consider revelation in abstraction from man as recipient.

From time to time he does seek to clarify his view that theology does not speak of revelation without speaking at the same time of man as the recipient of divine revelation. It would not be revelation if man were to remain outside the range of man's hearing. Since the circle of man's own existence is constantly intersected by the circle of revelation, these two cannot be separated.[9]

Early in *Church Dogmatics* Barth makes a distinction between an "essential" and a "factual" necessity:[10] The hearing of man is not an essential necessity to the concept of the Word of God, he says, but it must be posited as a factual necessity for the actual speaking of the Word of God in history. It is only by God's grace, however, that man is even co-posited as such with God. This is no ground upon which to build a natural theology. Barth thought that Bultmann was mistaken to

[81]

make the hearing of man an *essential* necessity to the speaking of God. God is under no necessity on his side, says Barth, but in practice he allows man to be included in the speaking-hearing dialogue.

Our question at present concerns the relation of the action of God to the action of man in the act of obedience. The simplest way to put the question is whether it is God or man who is the acting subject in the act of obedience.

Barth says that obedience involves man's own answer to the deed which God has done and the Word which he has spoken. As such it is both the free gift of grace, *God's action*, and the free decision of man, *man's action*. If it is not simultaneously a truly human act, and a truly divine gift, then Barth thinks that it cannot be what Christianity calls obedience to God. For such is the definition of obedience to God: man's self-determination under the divine predetermination. In the act of obedience, God allows his claim to be heard and man allows the command of God to lay claim to his own free, spontaneous self-determination. But in the midst of man's self-determination, the freedom of God never *competes* with the freedom of man. Rather, says Barth, obedience is precisely that relationship in which both God and man are truly free.

The content of the Word of God for the obedient man is always a most concrete demand (*concretissimum*). Like Bultmann, Barth says that God's command has no content if one tries to abstract it from the unique address of the living Word to the living man. The Word to which man is obedient is not an idea or an objective datum, nor any kind of nonhistorical notion of requirement. It is objective only in the sense that it is God's own self-presentation. As such it always has "a wholly special objective content" [11] in the moment. The divine concrete requirement can never be anticipated or repeated by man, nor conceived of or reproduced as a general truth.

The Good Deed. Man cannot, of himself, do the good which God does for him, but what he ought to do and can do is to determine that his action shall correspond to the action of God. In such an act of obedience, man allows himself to be included within the action of God. Such an act would never claim that an innate good lies resident within the human side of the action.

Barth subsumes the category of the "good" entirely under the category of obedience. "Therefore, man does *good* only insofar as he *hears* the Word of God, and *acts* as hearer of this Word. In this action as hearer, he is obedient. *Why is obedience good?* Because it derives from hearing. Because it is the action of a hearer, viz., the hearer of the Word of God. It is good *because the divine address is good,* because God himself is good." [12] The reason why the language of obedience is so important to Barth is that it provides a framework for understanding God as the doer of the good, without opening the door for man to consider the good as immanent within himself, while preserving the notion of free self-determination in man.

Man's answer to God's Word is a truly human answer, Barth insists. It is an answer which man himself gives, and no one else can give it for him. God does not mechanically prearrange man's response, but allows man to be a genuinely free Thou before him. But the good which is done in the obedient act belongs to God and not to man. The only goodness of which the Christian message speaks is "the goodness in which God acts toward man." [13] Man's action is good only insofar as it mirrors God's action.

For this reason, obedience can never take on the character of a "merit" or a "virtue." True obedience, says Barth, is "claimless obedience," [14] and seeks to lay no counterclaim upon God by virtue of itself. The content of God's command is simply that man should confirm in his circle of action what God has done in Christ. Man's action in the human circle remains human, but it can mirror, attest and affirm God's action.

The Freedom of God. The inquiry into Christian obedience, according to Barth, focuses upon man as he is determined by the reality of God's election and God's command. It is not spuriously free to wander into the consideration of other less palpable possibilities. Since it regards the command of God as a reality, it cannot treat it as a mere possibility. It can never subsume God's command under some higher ethical category. In the inquiry into Christian obedience, we can never finally "complete" our consideration of God's choice and then turn separately to an examination of man's choice, since in the act of obedience, these two determinations coincide.

What is good has been "said" to man already in Jesus Christ.[15] Man's task is to act in correspondence with the Word therein spoken. In inquiring into obedience, the theologian cannot begin by supposing that he first needs to discover what is the nature of the good before he can obey it. For he has already begun at a point prior to this, viz., the acknowledgment that the good has already been chosen in Jesus Christ. It is only in obedience to this choice of God that man can choose the good. He does not choose the good by choosing between good and evil, but only by obedience, i.e., acknowledging the good as already having been chosen. Man's choice must be: to choose the One who has chosen him. Man's only choice concerning the good is to say Yea or Nay to God's choice. Obedience means: to choose God's choice.

Barth does not hesitate, therefore, to say that in the last analysis man's own true freedom is "verily God's own freedom." [16] Any notion of the freedom of man which autonomously separates itself from God's own freedom destroys itself. The biblical witness, Barth thinks, is not concerned to protect some sort of freedom on man's side from encroachment by God. It speaks of freedom only as it exists out of God's grace, and in responsiveness to it.

In Jesus Christ, God has revealed himself as free "for man" as covenant partner. Man's action is always already included in the action of God, whether he acknowledges it or not. But how does man come to acknowledge it, and order his life in terms of it? Such is a possibility which lies not with man, but only with the Holy Spirit. It is only in connection with the action of God the Holy Spirit, Barth thinks, that we may properly speak of "the human side" of obedience.

C. The Holy Spirit as Instructor in Sensitivity

Be Who You Are! Christian ethics operates on the indicative-imperative: we must be who we *are*.[17] Who man *is*, as one justified by God, determines what he must *do*. The work of God the Holy Spirit, as man's instructor in sensitivity, consists in continually setting man on his feet as an authentic man and permitting him to be free as such. The Holy Spirit does not offer man a general new *possibility*, the actualization of which is man's duty. Rather, he provides the new presupposition for true human action: the reality of the new man. It is under the teleological power of this presupposition that man acts obediently.

The Holy Spirit does not "make man an offer" or "give man a chance" to be obedient, or "command a possible action" to man.[18] The Holy Spirit is distinguished from other "spirits" in that he corrects the presupposition for man's entire existence, and provides the new being out of which obedient doing eventuates. He bestows upon man a unique point of departure, his authentic humanity, and allows him the freedom to be who he is. Use of the freedom is obedience. All of man's previous attempts to decide for good and evil become one long innovation in the light of this new presupposition for decision.

The new man finds himself placed under a strict command, and a correspondingly strict prohibition. He is commanded to make use of the freedom for which he has been set free. The prohibition requires that he not make use of that spurious freedom which acts out of the erroneous presupposition that he is not a covenant partner with God.

Man for Himself. God the Spirit places man at this particu-

[85]

lar point of departure where he has only one path ahead: being who he is. Other "spirits" may be distinguished from the Holy Spirit by the way in which they offer man many possibilities for his choosing. They do not really trust man's freedom, and therefore do not place him at a wholly new beginning point.

The Holy Spirit is in one way wholly for man, and in another way wholly against him. He summons man to be wholly *for himself* by being wholly against the inauthentic self who starts at the negated beginning point. He works against man insofar as man is against himself. The responsive man, under the pedagogy of the Spirit, is continually directed away from any compromise or balance of power which might be proposed between the new and old man.

The Spirit and the Situation. Barth argues that the Holy Spirit directs and orients the obedient man in a wholly definite way "in every time and in every place and in every situation." [19] In God's manifold commands, however, it is always one and the same command that he gives to man: to become who he is, as reconciled, redeemed, forgiven and justified. In the face of being confronted by many possibilities, the Spirit gives man the single option: his new creaturehood in Jesus Christ.

The Holy Spirit does not instruct man by laying down general rules or principles of action, Barth says, but by actually instructing man in the objective here and now to the end that he may in every situation be who he is. "He is the One—and this is his instruction—who actually discloses and makes known the will of God as it applies to us concretely in our here and now. He imparts and writes on our hearts and conscience the command of God in the individual and specific form in which we have to deal with it in our situation." [20] The Holy Spirit does not give man "general" knowledge of what he is to do, leaving considerable room for the interpretation of details, Barth believes, since it is the details which matter the most. Rather, he gives man the most specific instruction for the most concrete obedience. Man's moral reasoning cannot generalize

he directives of the Spirit so that they could be adequately
ummarized in a written code or universal principle.

The particularized instructions of the Holy Spirit, as exem-
lified in the New Testament exhortations, often intersect
nd seemingly contradict one another. Barth regards this as a
witness to the freedom of the Holy Spirit. But in all his mani-
old addressing, the single instruction of the Spirit in each
oncrete situation is to awaken man to the freedom for which
e has been set free.[21]

Similar to Bultmann's idea of the discernibility of the demand of God, Barth declares that it belongs to the nature of
he Word of God to be apprehensible to man. But the way in
which the Word is apprehended, Barth insists, is through the
work of the Holy Spirit. It is God himself as Holy Spirit who
ives men ears to hear his Word. "The Lord who speaks is
he Lord of our hearing. The Lord who gives the Word is the
Lord who gives faith. The Lord of our hearing is, by his act
f making man truly and actually open and ready for the
Word (not another God but the one God), the Holy
pirit." [22]

Man does not hear the command of God by his own in-
enuity or attentiveness, but by the work of God himself,
hrough the Holy Spirit. All of man's believing, hearing and
beying receives its possibility only from God. The event of
uman hearing is a truly human event, but it is never a
manipulable process lying within man's control.

D. Freedom for Life and for the Neighbor

The Command to Live. What is the content of the command of God the Creator to man as creature?

Responsibility to God the Creator requires something very
imple of man: that he *live!* The Creator gives man life, and
n doing so asks (and therefore permits) man to live—to
ccept life with joy and to affirm and reverence life itself. Not

[87]

that life as such is to become an idol, as a second God, or something to be reverenced in itself, but that life should and may be regarded as a gift of God, or, as Barth suggests, a "lien." The very fact that man exists carries with it the explicit command that man may and should exist. Man has been given permission to live, and the command of God simply requires that he make use of that permission.[23]

It is especially in the light of the Incarnation that man is enabled to rejoice in life as a gift. For therein, God himself affirms human existence by entering it. In Jesus Christ, God declares that human life is good by living as a man. Since obedience to God consists in determining oneself according to the good which God has chosen, man is called to receive his own life as good. The Decalogue's injunction "Thou shalt not kill" is interpreted positively by Barth to mean "Thou shalt live!" It enjoins "reverence for life," [24] both for one's own life and for the lives of others.

But obedience to God the Creator requires, conversely, that man accept and rejoice in the *limitation* which is implicit in the sheer fact that he is creature and not Creator, man and not God. His life is limited to a fleeting span of years which constitute a definite opportunity, albeit an opportunity with a definite boundary: death. The obedience of man as creature involves the acknowledgment of the boundary as the gift of God. The accent should fall upon the Giver of the opportunity, rather than despair over the boundary ahead. Obedience to God means the affirmation of the divine circumscribing of life, not as a tyrannical limitation, accident or curse, but as gift and opportunity.

All obedience to God takes place within the sphere of this divine limitation. Man is man precisely under the condition of this limitation, and thus the freedom which belongs to man belongs to him only in the context of this limitation. Human obedience in the face of death involves not only the acknowledgment of death as a boundary, but as God's boundary.[25]

Man may live confidently within these boundaries, Barth

declares, since God has won his confidence by himself sharing these boundaries. In Jesus Christ man sees God becoming obediently subject to all these boundaries.

He who takes this vantage point no longer stands in an abstract relationship to his present and future, Barth declares. He is enabled to be continually open to the future and decisive in the present. The man who is obedient to the command "to live," says Barth, does not live as an impersonal nonentity, but as an integrate "I." He is not an other-directed man, looking to the crowd around him for the canons of right action. He stands in the midst of other men and their concrete needs, receiving the moment as a gift and their needs as a command. He is called to govern his time responsibly, in the knowledge that he will not have an unlimited amount of time.

Vocation. In obedience to God the Creator, man acknowledges that he finds himself in a particular historical situation which has already been assigned to him, and in which he knows himself to be assigned to the needs of his neighbors. His *vocation* is the station in life in which he finds his place of responsibility under God's command. Man is called to freedom within the limits of his vocation.

Barth distinguishes between obedience to a calling (*Berufung*) and obedience in a vocation (*Beruf*). Calling always refers to a specific event which calls man to a particular activity. Vocation refers not merely to man's vocational work (*Berufsarbeit*) but more exactly to the whole of man's existence under the calling of God, and to man's special realm of responsibility in which he finds himself under the calling of God. Thus *man's vocation always presupposes God's calling.*[26] It should be clear that man is never called to be obedient to his vocation, but only to God in the concrete demands of his vocation. Barth warns against certain Lutheran interpretations that tend to make an idolatry out of vocation itself. One does not necessarily need to remain in a particular vocation in his obedience to God's call.

Fellowship-Humanity. It belongs to man's existence to

be *with* other men (*Mitmenschlichkeit*). Barth resembles G. H. Mead and Martin Buber in his view of the self—that man cannot be man without his fellow men. Barth's view of *Mitmenschlichkeit*, or, one might say, "fellowship-humanity," is distinctive, however, in its insistence that in Jesus Christ we find the pattern of *the man for other men.*[27]

The need of man to be *with* his fellow man is inalienable to man's true nature. It is the *sine qua non* of humanity, and not something added on to our created nature *à la* Hobbes or Rousseau. Barth admits that the Christian view of human selfhood shares this conception of fellowship-humanity with others outside the church, such as Buber the Jew, Feuerbach the atheist, and Confucius.[28] But it is only in the man Jesus that we find the profoundest clarification of our fellowship-humanity, i.e., as grounded in the election of God. It is from this perspective that the church speaks of a humanity which is common to Christian and non-Christian—the covenant humanity which finds its fulfillment and clarification in Jesus Christ.

In speaking of "the man for other men," Barth does not simply mean that Jesus served and loved other men, but much more that his humanity had its very existence in relation to other men, and that his human *being* was in its very heart bound up with the being of his fellows. As we cannot understand health from sickness, we cannot understand man's true humanity from the point of view of his inhumanity, and we cannot understand his true nature from the perspective of his isolation and loneliness.[29]

Man and Woman. The basic pattern of fellowship-humanity is the relation of man and woman. Like the relation of Yahweh and Israel in the covenant, man and woman confront one another both in their differences and in their "belonging together."[30] The basic pattern of man's relation to others is one of mutual need and mutual interdependence.

Man is not truly man without woman, nor is woman truly woman without man. The command of God, in its sexual reference, requires and permits man and woman to be truly man and truly woman. Obedience to the command of the Creator requires that they make use of this permission.

The command implies a limitation. Man is limited to his maleness and woman to her femaleness, and the overstepping of these limitations is a flight into inhumanity. In order to be obedient as a sexual being, man must render account to his sexual companion. Any turning away from woman as companion is regarded by Barth as disobedience to God. From this follows Barth's argument against homosexuality.

All obedience to God takes place within the framework of the covenant relationship. But Barth regards the covenant relationship not exclusively as a relation between God and man, but analogously as a relation between man and his fellow man. The exemplary form of this covenant between man and his fellow man is the existence together of man and woman, in their differentiation and in their reference to one another.[31]

E. The Horizontal Continuity
of God's Command

Vertical and Horizontal. How does Barth's view of obedience escape the charges of fanaticism, spiritualism and solipsism? Such inferences might conceivably be drawn from what has been said about the particularity and concreteness of the demand and the guidance of the Holy Spirit.

In speaking in this way Barth notes that he does not mean to imply that the man of obedience is dependent from one moment to the next on individual "special revelations." Nor, on the other hand, does he wish to set up such a rigid notion of continuity that it might run the danger of legalism, such as the idea of "orders of creation" might. Barth thought that Brunner's *Divine Imperative* was not careful enough to avoid either one of these opposite types of fanaticism.

The obedient act is not merely a vertical encounter of God's command and man in the moment, but it is always simultaneously a horizontal encounter of man with other men in a durable history. The vertical encounter never takes place in abstraction from a historical context. There is no vertical command and no vertical obedience which can be abstracted from the continuity of the divine demanding. But the continuity is God's continuity, not man's. The only horizontal dimension of Christian obedience is the horizontal continuity of God's eternal Word, penetrating the uniqueness of every moment.[32]

From this vantage point Barth rejects both Brunner's view of the orders of creation and Bonhoeffer's view of the divine mandates. There is a continuity in human history and society, Barth argues, but this continuity is wholly dependent upon "the steadiness and continuity of the divine commands." [33] The horizontal sphere never possesses an imperative in itself.

To be sure, man certainly does not live in a purely "vertical" sphere, as if he were "out of history," Barth declares. Rather, the horizontal and vertical always intersect, and become what they are in relation to one another. The horizontal sphere is the spatio-temporal "place" in which the command of God becomes visible. The vertical dimension would be wholly abstract without the horizontal.

The Continuity of the Covenant. One is never called to be obedient *to* the horizontal orders of human existence, Barth says, but always to *God* within these orders. Barth's quarrel with the traditional "orders of creation" is essentially that they make the orders an independent force or entity which can be considered abstractly, apart from the fact that they are *God's* orders.

Likewise, one is never called to be obedient *to* the moment, or to the demand of the moment, but always to *God* in the moment. Barth's quarrel with Bultmann's "radical obedience" is essentially his contention that Bultmann has made an idolatry of the moment. The moment must not be considered abstractly, apart from the Lord of the moment.[34]

Although he rejects the scholastic Lutheran "orders of creation," Barth speaks of certain horizontal orders (*Ordnungen*) of human existence which form the framework for human obedience. He never defines these orders as independent or neutral spheres, but he simply refers to them as the area or realm (*Bereich*) of the divine commanding and the corresponding human obeying.[35] The divine demand does not meet man in a vacuum, but in the historical, horizontal, human, temporal, experiential realm where man lives.

The predominant emphasis of Barth's social ethics is not the theme of the continuity of political and social orders, as if these orders had some sort of autonomous status in nature apart from grace. Rather, the locus of continuity is always, for Barth, in God, and never in the orders themselves. The horizontal sphere in which human obedience takes place has no existence in and of itself, but only out of grace.

Disobedience to God is, from man's point of view, a breaking of the continuity of the covenant relation. But from God's point of view the continuity is never broken. In spite of every human interruption, the horizontal continuity of the divine commanding and reconciling remains uninterrupted. The real continuities of human existence are maintained not by man but by God's grace. In Jesus Christ he has declared his decision that his faithfulness shall not be put to nought by man's unfaithfulness.

F. The Ontological Impossibility of Disobedience

The Choice. The freedom of the Christian man does not consist in a choice between two or more possibilities, but between a possibility and an impossibility, Barth writes. When man chooses to be disobedient to grace, he is choosing the absurd, the impossible and the groundless. He is choosing what God has negated, and therefore is without ontological grounding.[36]

Man's *only* ontological possibility, as true man, is to be free to be who he *is*, to be God's covenant partner. Disobedience consists in the human attempt vainly to make real and historical that which is ontologically impossible.[37] To be sure, man does in fact constantly try to realize this ontological impossibility, and herein is the essence of his sin. But the fact that man is a sinner does not give sin an ontological status in creation. Why does man disobey?

Barth takes the position that we cannot explain the origin of disobedience, not because we are limited in our thinking, but because disobedience is itself absurd, enigmatic and inexplicable. We must not ever give the fact of human sin a permanent, inevitable or legitimate place in creation, since creation is fully good and in it there is intended to be no *real* room for disobedience to God.[38]

Man's disobedience cannot be deduced from his nature, which *as* God's creation is good. Nor can we say that the root of man's disobedience is freedom, since the original freedom of the authentic man is a freedom which is given the sole ontological possibility of being for God. To the question "Why is man disobedient to God's grace!" the only proper answer can be silence.[39]

When Barth speaks of disobedience as "the ontological impossibility of human existence," [40] he means that man has no ground upon which to stand, ontologically, in his rebellion against God's grace. Disobedience to God can never really *be* —it is absurd and impossible, ontologically. Man actually does disobey, of course, but in doing so he does that which is impossible for him as he *actually* is, i.e., as a new creature in Jesus Christ. Disobedience is a fact, but it is a groundless fact. Disobedience is a possibility only if we look at man in and for himself, from man's side. But such a perspective Barth regards as abstract, in that man is taken out of the covenant relation to which he belongs.

The Divine Negation. The covenant relation is the first thing that must be predicated about man, before man's disobedience to the covenant relation is to be predicated. Likewise man's disobedience cannot be the last thing said about him. For his disobedience and rebellion take place only, so to speak, in a kingdom in which grace resigns unassailably.

To be a man means primarily, in Barth's view, to be chosen by God, to be elected to covenant existence. Thus covenant is prior to creation. Grace is prior to man's fallenness. To be a man means from the outset to be utterly dependent upon God's creating grace, for no man has within himself even the slightest potentiality for calling himself into existence.

When Barth speaks of disobedience to God as an ontological impossibility, he means that rebellion against God's grace is something which in the very nature of the case cannot "be." It has no being because God has said No to it.[41] Man, who has not established the covenant relation, cannot destroy it, try as he may. In his disobedience, man seeks to choose that which, as covenant partner, he cannot choose. He tries to affirm that which God has negated, and thus disobedience is finally an ontological impossibility.[42]

Epilogue:
Barth and the Future of Christian Ethics

We are not proposing that Barth's ethical perspective is fully adequate for the whole range of agonizing questions which trouble contemporary Christian ethicists. Rather, we are suggesting that at the center of that broad circumference, viz., with respect to our preconditioning assumptions and in our examination of our theological axioms for Christian action, Barth has something to say which has never been adequately heard. We are further convinced that what he has to say is profoundly akin to the emerging secular mentality in ways which may be surprising to those who have already consigned him to the oblivion of a past era.

Surely it must be admitted from the outset that many readers will not wish to buy all of Barth's categories and assumptions. Much of what he says will be viewed as archaic, quaint and inapplicable to the contemporary situation. Surely it must be clear to readers who are familiar with my other writings that I myself am no slavish Barthian scholastic. This book is not written out of a backward-looking "neo-orthodox" mentality, nor does it propose that Barth's viewpoint should be bought wholesale in an uncritical way. Yet we do wish to set before the reader this viewpoint as a potentially promising option for the future reflection of Christians on man's moral existence.

There can be no doubt that in our era man is struggling for a fresh, meaningful redefinition of his own humanity. Barth's discussion of "authentic man" deserves to figure in this re-appraisal. Why? Because he is proposing that humanity is God's gift, never to be ungiven. Man's possibility and task is to discover ever anew that he shares this covenant humanity, and to appropriate that discovery in his behavior.

Without any phoniness, what is Barth saying to us today? He is saying: You are being called simply to become who you are, to actualize your own humanity. You are not being asked to do something that is alien to your actual being.

Do not mistake this for a romanticist naturalism which says: Moral behavior is sheer, spontaneous, unique self-expression. However valuable that may be, that is not quite Barth's point. Rather, he is saying: You *are* a covenant partner with God. You *are* the recipient of grace. You *are* one whose life is given and whose freedom is enabled by God. Therefore be who you are. Be that person. Actualize the unique possibility which is before you of being a fully functioning, mature human being.

What is so promising about this orientation? I experience as profoundly the healing realization that what I am called to do is merely to actualize my deepest being, and that my deepest being does not finally depend upon my own choosing of it, but upon God's own choosing of me.

That is an arresting viewpoint, a fresh alternative. In a hidden sense it seems to be in harmony with the spirit of the emerging generation, with its call to self-disclosure, personal authenticity, and protest against alien legalisms and its demand for contextual relevance. Barth's ethic is potentially geared to just that emerging life style.

Nowhere is that life style more dramatically epitomized than in our current struggle to understand ourselves as sexual partners. If the emerging generation hears nothing from Barth except his view of the relation of man and woman, that will be of immense benefit. For he is saying to you that you exist as a sexual being, and therefore that your existence is bound up in covenant community, so that you do not fully understand yourself if you see yourself in terms of some abstract

[97]

individualism, i.e., as an individuated sexual being. If you are a woman, your womanhood is fulfilled in relation to man. If you are a man, then your very being as a man is fulfilled only in relation to woman. Nothing is more concretely expressive of man's covenant relationship than is sexual intimacy, and most specifically, orgasm. For as surely as man and woman run to meet each other and fulfill each other in their mutual differences and in their being together, so it is that human beings as a whole need each other in their daily interactions to fulfill their covenant humanity. Your humanity is not completed just in itself, but in relation to others whose needs you fulfill and who fulfill your needs.

Young people today are searching for a more profound, more moral conception of sexuality. Already this generation is learning that sexuality points beyond itself to our fundamental human interdependence, and thus in a certain sense to our essential being as covenant man. At just that point, the Christian ethic, especially as grasped by Barth, addresses the contemporary discussion on sexuality with a new and liberating word about the new man, viz., that the pattern for man's being together with his neighbor is finally clarified in the pattern of God's own being with man and for man in the history of the people of Israel. God loves and cares for Israel even in spite of Israel's rejection of that love. Analogously, we are being called to love and care for the neighbor, even and precisely in the midst of his rejection and mistrust of that caring love.

Conclusions and Prospectus

Our chief findings may be summarized in three points:

(1) In answer to the question "What is obedience to God?" Barth insisted that we focus strictly on the content of the gospel, which declares that Jesus Christ is obedient in our place. Man is called to acknowledge and attest in his activity this electing grace of God. The only basis of the divine claim is grace. God has authenticated his claim by showing himself to be "for us" in the Christ event. The Christian ethic does

not begin with the assertion that man must take responsibility for himself, but, rather, with the proclamation that God has taken responsibility for man.

(2) The command of God simply requires that man become who he is as the recipient of God's reconciling action. Its special form is permission, commanding man to make use of the freedom for which he is set free. The command of God does not confront man with many possibilities, but with the single possibility that he may be who he is, free for God and his neighbor. Responsive and sensitive listening to this command in all its situational concreteness constitutes genuine freedom.

(3) The command of God corrects the presupposition for man's entire existence and provides the new being out of which the new doing eventuates. The form of the responsible act is once for all seen and recognized in the true man, the man for others, Jesus Christ. Man's lack of accountability to the reality at hand has the character of absurdity. It is without grounding in the nature of things, and thus nothing more than man's impossible attempt to affirm that which God has negated. These three points constitute the basic themes of chapters II, III and IV, above.

The essential contributions of Barth's thought to the current discussion of Christian ethics may be summarized in these points:

(1) Barth is suggesting a new direction for an ethic of self-realization by his theological redefinition of the self, i.e., he has taken the familiar ethical dictum, "Become who you are!" and has reconceived the "you" to be "you, the covenant partner," "you, the recipient of grace in Christ," "you, the one who has been met by God's reconciling action."

(2) Barth's reversal of the classical law and gospel theme, emphasizing the priority of gospel to law, is a promising direction for current Christian ethics now trying to work through the issues of "law and order," revolution and social legitimation.

(3) Not since Calvin has Protestantism seen such a thoroughgoing attempt to base the concept of human responsibility on the prior question of the responsibility of God for man.

(4) Barth's insistence that man is wholly self-determined while being simultaneously under the total determination of the command of God constitutes a unique solution to the perennial problem of human freedom and divine necessity.

(5) Barth's view that authentic human freedom cannot be misused, but only used or not used, and that responsibility is merely the *use* of freedom, and that the special form of the command of grace is permission, constitutes a fresh new perspective on the meaning of freedom.

(6) Barth's interpretation of biblical legislation, e.g., the Sabbath commandment as permission, is a highly suggestive interpretive procedure for studies in biblical ethics.

(7) The notion of the ontological impossibility of disobedience is imaginative, provocative and full of unexplored ramifications.

Why have we chosen ethics as the focus of our discussion of the promise of Barth? For two reasons: (1) Even by his most astute interpreters, Barth's ethics has been neglected. It is consistently regarded as the weaker aspect of his contribution, and often viewed as the least promising dimension. (2) In the light of this it is ironic that one of the most salvageable aspects of Barth's work after the deluge of secularization is his ethics. We are proposing that it is precisely his ethics which has special relevance for the emerging situation.

It may appear to some that Barth's viewpoint is jaded and parochial, inasmuch as he seems to have contented himself with using traditional language to speak to traditional Christians. It must be acknowledged that Barth has been much less interested in the question of communication with the contemporary mind than he has with the question of God's own self-communication. Barth is vulnerable to the charge that he has refused to accommodate his categories to the assumptions

of the contemporary mind. That has hardly been one of his
virtues as a theologian.

Thus it becomes necessary to ask: How are those outside the
Christian tradition (including many who are nominally within
it) to take Barth? Does he merely display an enclave mentality, a ghetto frame of reference, which is only relevant to those
who share his special presuppositions?

Barth's answer is worth hearing: Honest dialogue cannot
afford to dilute or hide one's axiomatic assumptions. It must
listen to the neighbor, and always entertain the possibility of
revising even its assumptions, but it must be congruent in-
wardly and candid outwardly about the ground upon which
it stands. For example, in Christian-Marxist dialogue, it does
not help the process of genuine communication for either side
to pretend that they have no assumptions which they bring to
the dialogue. For the Christian community, the central assumption out of which their whole reflective process emerges
is the assumption that God has met us in Jesus Christ. Barth
has not encouraged any sort of cheap and self-deceptive dialogue which pretends to "leave behind one's central assumptions in order presumably to accord the partner a fair hearing."
For to really hear the partner is to hear him as one who is
being met, whether he recognizes and celebrates it or not, by
the same reality which is confessed and celebrated in Christian
worship.

On the other hand, Barth himself has spent his career in
vigorous and meaningful dialogue with options radically different from his own. He has taken his critics with immense
seriousness, but in a very special way, and with a particular
understanding of the dialogical process: Every erroneous statement has a dialectical element of truth in it. The task of the
critical man is to attempt to hear the hidden truth which is
present in the speech of the partner in dialogue. For Barth, let
us add, it is clear that the most profound truth hidden in any
human dialogue is the truth which is finally made known in

Jesus Christ. So, whether in dialogue with the psychotherapist, the Hindu, the Marxist or whomever, one is listening intently for nothing less than the self-disclosure of man's covenant humanity. That may sound as if dialogue is reduced merely to listening for those aspects of the partner's speech with which one already agrees. But that misses the point slightly. For dialogue with alternative life styles means to seek to hear *within* the special framework of the partner's viewpoint, whether theist or atheist, Oriental or Westerner, revolutionary or anarchist, the hidden elements of man's genuine humanity already yearning for fuller self-disclosure.

So the whole concept of dialogue itself is transformed to mean not merely speaking and listening to one another, but, even more, speaking and listening to each other in such a way that we may hear God's own speech present in our speaking and hearing. That is rather different from ordinary notions of dialogue. This view is beautifully stated by Barth in his previously cited letter to East German Christians who were seeking his counsel on how to dialogue with the overt atheism of their social system: ". . . you should accept none of your countrymen at their own estimate. Don't ever honor them as the unbelieving and strong men they pretend to be! . . . They are just posing as the strong men they would like to be! Rather, you must meet their unbelief with a joyous unbelief in their attempted atheism. You as Christians must confidently claim that your atheists belong to God as much as you do. Whether they will be converted . . . is a secondary question. What is certain is that God is not against them, but for them." [1]

Notes

Chapter I. Why Karl Barth?

1. *Time*, April 20, 1962.
2. *Die Christliche Dogmatik im Entwurf* (München: Christian Kaiser, 1927), p. ix. This translation is from Paul Lehmann, "The Changing Course of a Corrective Theology," *Theology Today*, Oct. 1956, p. 334.
3. John McConnachie, *The Significance of Karl Barth* (London: Richard R. Smith, 1931), p. 43.
4. Quoted in the *New York Times*, December 10, 1968.
5. *The Knowledge of God and the Service of God* (London: Hodder and Stoughton, 1938), p. 221.
6. Quoted in B. A. Willems, O.P., *Karl Barth, An Ecumenical Approach to His Theology* (Glen Rock, N.J.: Paulist Press, 1965), p. 48.
7. *Community, State and Church*, ed. W. Herberg (New York: Doubleday, 1960), p. 40.
8. *How to Serve God in a Marxist Land* (New York: Association Press, 1959), pp. 57–58.
9. *Against the Stream* (London: SCM Press, 1954), p. 40.
10. *Evangelical Theology: An Introduction* (New York: Holt, Rinehart and Winston, 1963), p. xii.
11. Helmut Thielicke, *Theological Ethics*, Vol. I, ed. W. Lazareth (Philadelphia: Fortress Press, 1966), pp. 98, 108, 113; R. R. Niebuhr, *Resurrection and Historical Reason* (New York: Scribners, 1957), pp. 73, 146; Joseph Fletcher, *Situation Ethics* (Philadelphia: Westminster Press, 1966), pp. 62, 149–150.
12. John Baillie, *Our Knowledge of God* (New York: Scribners, 1959), pp. 187–188.
13. Thielicke, *op. cit.*, pp. 322–333.
14. R. R. Niebuhr, *op. cit.*, p. 50.
15. John Cobb, *Living Options in Protestant Theology* (Philadelphia: Westminster Press, 1962), p. 173.
16. Reinhold Niebuhr, *Christianity and Crisis*, XIX, 101; *Essays in Applied Christianity*, ed. D. B. Robertson (New York: Living Age Books, 1959), pp. 186, 172.
17. For a recent, concise, but substantial discussion of Barth's ethics which avoids caricature, see James M. Gustafson, *Christ and the Moral Life* (New York: Harper & Row, 1968).

Chapter II. Christ's Obedience and Ours

1. *Church Dogmatics*, Volume II, Part 2 (Edinburgh: T. & T. Clark, 1957), p. 542. Hereafter, references to *Church Dogmatics* will follow the conventional style of citation for this work, e.g., II/2, 542.

2. II/2, 579.
3. III/4, 350ff.
4. II/2, 538–539.
5. II/2, 539–540.
6. IV/2, 511–533, 620.
7. IV/2, 511ff.
8. IV/2, 513; 52ff; IV/1, 157ff.
9. "Gospel and Law," in *Community, State and Church, op. cit.*
10. II/2, 511. Italics added.
11. I/1, 233.
12. I/1, 229.
13. I/1, 226–234. Barth is here enjoying the benefits and suffering under
the inadequacies of the Kantian understanding of freedom. Kant insisted that
freedom and law reciprocally imply each other, and that *freedom means nothing other than the will which is subject to reason's moral law.*

Kant had the greatest confidence that the voice of moral reason was unambiguous, "distinct," "irrepressible," and "clearly audible" in every man,
"even the commonest man." If this were not the case, then morality, he
thought, would be in complete ruin. His moral thought operated on the grand
presupposition of the Enlightenment that, since all men are basically rational,
and the reasoning of one man corresponds with the reasoning of all men
universally, knowledge of the moral demand is resident and distinct in every
man alike. He did not think that it was ever beyond man's power to answer
and fulfill the simple demands of the categorical imperative, to "act on that
maxim which I can will as universal law." Kant writes, "The decision as to
what is to be done in accordance with the categorical imperative must not be
so difficult that even the commonest and most unpracticed understanding
without any worldly prudence should go wrong in making it." *Critique of
Practical Reason,* tr. L. W. Beck (New York: The Liberal Arts Press, 1956),
p. 38 (italics mine).

Kant thought that he had captured the essence of the rational demand
in its simplest form: I must simply act on that maxim which I can conscien-
tiously will as a universal law for all men. He thought that the rational will
would be determined objectively by this imperative, and subjectively it would
be determined by reverence for it. The demand is the same for any man in any
situation. What reason demands is not vague, Kant says. Everyone knows it,
if they would only attend to it. Another way of stating the same basic imperative is that I act so as to treat humanity (whether oneself or another) in
every case as an end in itself, and never as a means only.
14. II/2, 491ff.
15. I/1, 106.
16. II/2, 567.
17. II/2, 548, 556–568.
18. II/2, 511–512; cf. "Gospel and Law," *op. cit.* The Chalcedonian
formula indirectly provides a structural basis for Barth's view of the Christian
ethic centering upon the unity of the divine and human determinations. For
in the obedient act there is present truly God and truly man, distinct and
unconfused, and yet inseparable. One might suggest, however, in an analogical
fashion, that Barth occasionally falls into an ethical monophysitism by not

fully allowing the obedient act to be truly human, and by so emphasizing the absolute priority of the predetermination of God that the self-determination of man is sometimes unclear or neglected.

19. I/1, 171.
20. II/2, 553.
21. II/2, 555.
22. II/2, 556. Cf. Bultmann's view that the deed of God in the Christ event "gives us the right to believe in the God in whom we would fain believe."
23. IV/1, sec. 57.
24. II/2, 557–559.
25. II/2, 560.
26. II/2, 562f.
27. "Gospel and Law," *op. cit.*
28. *Ibid.*; cf. *Die Kirchliche Dogmatik*, IV/4 (Zürich, EVZ-Verlag, 1967), pp. 129–131.
29. II/2, 562.
30. II/2, 563.
31. II/2, 572.
32. II/2, 565.
33. *Ibid.*

Chapter III. The Command of God: A Situation Ethic?

1. II/2, 519–20.
2. IV/1, sec. 57; cf. IV/4, 142–149.
3. Barth regards Rudolf Bultmann as the prime example of a contemporary theologian who, despite other achievements, makes the pivotal error of beginning with a general anthropology, *Dasein als "vorgläubiges,"* an ontology of human existence prior to faith (I/1, 36).
4. I/1, 2–3, 39.
5. I/2, 414–415.
6. II/2, 564ff.
7. II/2, 565.
8. I/2, 365.
9. IV/2, 540.
10. IV/2, 541ff.
11. IV/2, 542.
12. IV/2, 534.
13. I/1, 19.
14. II/2, 583.
15. Friedrich Schleiermacher, *Werke, Die christliche Sitte* (Berlin: Verlag G. Reimer, 1884), pp. 502ff.
16. IV/2, 536–539.
17. II/2, 517.
18. IV/2, 367.
19. IV/2, 411.
20. III/2, 132ff; III/3, 308ff; IV/2, 404ff.

21. III/1, 259–263; IV/4, 3ff.
22. III/4, 47–49; II/2, sec. 37.
23. II/2, 585.
24. III/4, 50f.
25. III/4, 58–67.
26. II/2, 588.
27. II/2, 579, 585–589, 594; cf. col. 2.
28. II/2, 594–597.
29. II/2, 576, 566ff.
30. II/2, 579.
31. II/2, 566–587; cf. IV/4, 144ff.
32. II/2, 586.
33. II/2, 566; IV/2, 366–367.

Chapter IV. Human Responsibility

1. III/2, 6ff.; 19–25; I/1, 40f. Or, man as God has chosen him to be, the man of God's own choosing.
2. III/2, 26.
3. IV/2, 266.
4. II/2, 541.
5. *Ibid.*
6. I/2, 370.
7. II/2, 516.
8. II/2, 517.
9. I/2, 362–364.
10. I/1, 158.
11. I/1, 159.
12. II/2, 546. Italics added.
13. II/2, 547.
14. II/2, 579.
15. II/2, 538.
16. I/2, 205.
17. IV/2, 363.
18. IV/2, 362–365.
19. IV/2, 373.
20. IV/2, 372.
21. IV/2, 375–377.
22. I/1, 207–208.
23. III/4, 324ff.
24. III/4, 328–334.
25. III/4, 565ff.
26. III/4, 595ff., 740f.
27. III/2, 285ff.
28. III/2, 277.
29. III/2, 208, 227f., 264f.
30. III/4, 117ff.; III/2, 294.
31. III/2, 139, 159, 169ff.

32. III/2, 17–27.
33. III/4, 17.
34. III/4, 18f., 370.
35. III/4, 38ff.
36. III/2, 132–134.
37. III/2, 197.
38. III/2, 27ff.
39. III/2, 30.
40. III/2, 136; IV/3, 438ff.
41. III/2, 34f., 41, 146–157, 434ff.
42. III/2, 34–35, 136.

Epilogue: Barth and the Future of Christian Ethics

1. *How To Serve God in a Marxist Land,* with Johannes Hamel (New York: Association Press, 1959), pp. 57–58.

Selected Bibliography
of Works by Karl Barth

The Epistle to the Romans. London: Oxford University Press, 1933.

Theological Existence To-day! London: Hodder and Stoughton, 1933.

Church Dogmatics. Twelve volumes. Edinburgh: T. & T. Clark, 1936–1960.

The Church and the Political Problem of Our Day. New York: Charles Scribner's Sons, 1939.

The Knowledge of God and the Service of God. New York: Charles Scribner's Sons, 1939.

This Christian Cause. New York: The Macmillan Company, 1941.

The Church and the War. New York: The Macmillan Company, 1944.

Natural Theology (with Emil Brunner). London: Geoffrey Bles, 1946.

The Only Way. New York: Philosophical Library, 1947.

The Teaching of the Church Regarding Baptism. London: SCM Press, 1948.

Against the Stream. London: SCM Press, 1954.

The Word of God and the Word of Man. New York: Harper & Brothers (Torchbooks), 1957.

Christ and Adam: Man and Humanity in Romans 5. New York: Harper & Brothers, 1957, and New York: Collier Books (paperback), 1962.

Dogmatics in Outline. New York: Harper & Brothers (Torchbooks), 1959.

Christmas. Edinburgh: Oliver and Boyd, 1959.

Protestant Thought: From Rousseau to Ritschl. New York: Harper & Brothers, 1959.

How to Serve God in a Marxist Land (with Johannes Hamel). New York: Association Press, 1959.

Anselm: Fides Quaerens Intellectum. Richmond, Virginia: John Knox Press, 1960.

Community, State, and Church. Garden City, New York: Doubleday and Company (Anchor Books), 1960.

The Humanity of God. Richmond, Virginia: John Knox Press, 1960.

Deliverance to the Captives. New York: Harper & Brothers, 1961.

Theology and Church. New York: Harper & Row, 1962.

Karl Barth, Church Dogmatics, Selected and with an Introduction by Helmut Gollwitzer. New York: Harper & Row (Torchbooks), 1962.

Evangelical Theology: An Introduction. New York: Holt, Rinehart and Winston, 1963.

Revolutionary Theology in the Making: Barth-Thurneysen Correspondence, 1914–1925. Trans. James D. Smart. Richmond, Virginia: John Knox Press, 1964.

God Here and Now. New York: Harper & Row, 1964.